How To Prune, Train and Tie Rose Plants

How To Prune, Train and Tie Rose Plants

● ● ●

Tom Liggett

Direct inquiries to: tomliggett.net

ISBN-13: 9781547189526
ISBN-10: 1547189525

This book is dedicated to Becky Smith. I wrote it so that you will have something interesting to read, Becky.

I met you on a springtime gone,
In a garden
(In a dell).
A fitting place
For two like souls
To forge a bond unique.

This book is also dedicated to my wife, Blanche Weber Liggett.
Every word I write and every breath I take is for you, Blanche.

You brought sunshine
To my night.
You gave sweetness
To my dreams.

I offer my special thanks to Susan Weber. You are a great friend and student, Susan.

A sister made
By marriage ink.
Friends built from garden dirt.

That basic stuff
Does make us all.
Love cements the deal.

My thoughts go out to Stephen Scanniello. You are doing it right, Stephen. You are a source of inspiration to us all. Thank you very much, for what you do with the rose.

Known by word
(Not much in person),
His pictures look sublime.
I'm certain ink
Does not do justice
To his legacy, divine.

Finally, I offer my humble regards to Milovan Milutin. Milovan was there through some of my biggest garden successes—and failures. Thank you, Milovan.

Ancient darkness
Creeps on me-
Steals away my dreams.

Ancient friendships
Bring me light-
Awaken bright new days.

Contents

Introduction

● ● ●

The hardest step,
Of ev'ry journey
Has always been the first.

That idea,
Is not my own
But it conveys my thoughts to you.

MOST OF THE PEOPLE WHO grow roses don't want to learn about history or theory. They just want to take care of the plants they have somehow accumulated. I celebrate those people. They are growing roses.

It doesn't require a lot of knowledge to grow rose plants. If suitable plants are given adequate sunlight, water, and fertilizer, they will generally explode with growth and bloom.

But there is an inevitable price that must be paid for growing vigorous plants; they must be pruned. Rose pruning requires a good amount of forethought and education. The nature of that education is not complex. Rose pruning is centered on one main concept: knowing how the plants grow.

This book will gently guide you through the ins and outs of rose biology. Worry not, gentle souls; I promise not to bury you in technical jargon.

I have included a glossary of terms in this book. Please refer to the glossary, if you want more data on a given topic. (Or if you want a good laugh.)

All good things came with caveats; this book has some, too. I do not claim to be a professional writer. The flaws in my literary skills are quite apparent in this tome.

What am I then? I am the last classically trained, full-spectrum professional rosarian who will ever be produced in the United States of America. I am the last link in a teacher-student chain that stretches back several hundred years. Some of you are probably thinking, "How can you know that is true, Tom?" Because the mechanism to create more like me no longer exists. Whole branches of the American rose industry have been eliminated. The great rose nurseries are gone. Most of the cut-flower greenhouses are gone. The great American rosarians are dead. The rose-growing hobby is almost nonexistent.

This eventuality has led me to a lonely place. There was a time wherein there were ten people such as me in every generation. I know that is true, because I lived in the waning days of those great times. Ah, it is sad to be the last of an ancient kind.

Please take the time to learn from my fifty-five-plus years as a professional gardener and rose pruner.

Garden Director Tom Liggett.

San Jose, California.

June 21, 2017.

An Introduction to the Theory of Pruning Rose Plants

● ● ●

Teacher, teacher,
Call on me!
I know the answer well.

Ah, my pupils,
Spoke the master
It goes deeper than you know.

I CAN TEACH ROSE-PRUNING THEORY via the written word. But I can't teach
rose-pruning mechanics in that fashion. Folks who want to prune roses
need to get outside and learn from the ground up.

I recommend you begin your quest for rose-pruning knowledge by
watching others prune roses. But there is an important trick contained in
that process; don't automatically assume the people you meet know anything about roses or how they should be pruned.

Everyone possesses differing levels of knowledge and experience.
Some casual rose growers are quite good at pruning their charges. Many
supposed experts don't prune roses correctly. This makes a confusing rec-
ipe for student pruners!

Most people who prune roses do so in their own gardens. From a
teaching perspective, that is the best way, in my opinion. The mistakes
you make on your own plants will be realized in dramatic ways.

Take extra care when you prune other people's roses. The pruning errors that you make on such plants might not be apparent to you.

If you are a neophyte pruner, please advise the plant owners of that fact. This should make them more forgiving of the mistakes you make. I hope their roses are, also.

When it comes to pruning, it is crucial that you venture cautiously. Don't prune any rose plant too severely. Once something is removed from a plant, it can't be glued back.

I have seen older plants die or sulk for years from a pruning mistake. I have also seen young, previously vigorous plants never recover from someone's misguided hack job.

WHAT MOST READERS WILL SEEK IN THIS BOOK

Most beginning rosarians want to learn just one thing: how to prune the rose bushes that are growing out in the yard. There is nothing wrong with that viewpoint. Simplicity of purpose should never be devalued.

START IN THE BUSH LEAGUES

Bush roses outnumber all other types by a factor of at least a hundred to one. That statistic should provide beginners with untold opportunities to become proficient at pruning bush roses.

But if you want to become a truly proficient pruner, I recommend you also learn about other types of roses. The lessons you learn from pruning old garden roses, shrubs, tree roses, or climbers will be invaluable when it comes to caring for regular ol' rose bushes.

ONE MILLION ROSE GROWERS, ONE MILLION DIVERSE PRUNING METHODS

I now grow most of my rose plants in San Jose, California. It seldom gets below 32 degrees Fahrenheit in our botanical paradise.

San Jose's benign climate is shared by less than 1 percent of the world's surface. In practical terms, this means San Jose is warmer in the winter and cooler in the summer than most other places where people grow roses.

Beyond climate, the greater San Francisco Bay Area is also unusual in another way; most of the people who live in our region were born somewhere else. This means many of the people who are gardening in the Bay Area are migratory gardeners. They came from other places, but they brought their rose-growing traditions with them to their new home.

If you are a recently transplanted gardener, I recommend you proceed slowly, until you figure out what is different about your new digs.

Take the Hippocratic oath

"First do no harm." Never were truer words written regarding treating people or pruning roses. Don't automatically assume that if a rose plant is sickly or overgrown, it needs to be pruned. Rose plants sometimes fare better when they are left unpruned. This is especially true when they get hacked by someone with good intentions and little experience.

If you aren't an experienced pruner, *don't* prune an overgrown rose plant. See "overgrown plant" in the glossary of terms.

Know why you're pruning roses

It is natural to assume other people are pruning roses with an appropriate quantity of knowledge and forethought. Sadly, that is not always the case. Most people prune roses in the manner that they were taught. That's not always the correct way.

The pruning methods people use might have been appropriate, way back home. Transplanted methods might not be beneficial when they move to a climate that has radically different growing and pruning requirements.

Your Aunt Tilly might well have been *the* ace rose pruner in Buffalo, New York. She might have taught you how to become a proficient pruner in your own right.

But San Jose, California, is a *long* way from Buffalo New York. So is Portland, Oregon, or Athens, Georgia, or Tyler, Texas. *Each* of those places have marked regional differences, in terms of what types of roses can be grown, and how they are pruned.

The punch line to this long-winded introduction is quite simple; venture cautiously in your rose-pruning endeavors.

WHO IS GIVING YOU ADVICE?

Don't automatically prune roses in ways other people say are correct. Why do I say that? Because I have observed a lot of rose gardeners. This makes me believe that a high percentage of the people in a pool of available teachers are *wrong* in their assumptions about rose pruning.

Process *any* advice that you receive about growing and pruning roses with great caution. You don't know how much knowledge and experience a potential advisor might have.

You should understand that knowledgeable pruners have definite jobs they wish to accomplish. They will prune in different styles.

For example, some rose-society members exhibit blooms to win prizes at rose shows. Don Marshall was one of the most successful rose exhibitors of all time. He said, "I don't care if a rose plant makes just two blooms a year, as long as one of them wins a ribbon."

Some exhibitors whack four-foot rose plants back to twelve-inch stubs. They believe such treatment will cause rose plants to produce larger blooms. I strongly disagree with that assumption. Larger plants usually have more leaves. Leaves create energy. Energy produces new growth and bloom.

Sadly, the "remove 75 percent of the plant" philosophy is shared by a high percentage of people who grow roses. This is because many gardeners learned how to prune roses in climates where roses must be covered to protect them from the ravages of very cold winters. See "winter protection" in the glossary of terms.

THE PUNCH LINE

I have pruned lots of roses for lots of people. Most of those people wanted me to cut their roses low. I always told them that their roses would do better if they were pruned high. Some folks listened to me. Some didn't. Then and now, I refuse to prune roses low. I missed out on a lot of pruning jobs, way back when.

When I was about thirty, I figured out that I was fighting a losing battle. I realized that everyone has strong opinions about pruning. One man can't counteract that much plant-hacking inertia. This has forced me to keep an open mind about the rose-pruning horrors and omissions that I witness.

DEAR NILES

Old rose plants of every description grow in the gardens of our town. They are leftovers from a bygone age. Many great rose nurseries were located within a couple of miles of my property. (The historic Leonard Coates nursery was located *on* my property.)

I formerly passed by a plant of Niles Cochet that was planted in about 1910. It survived over hundred years of booming development in downtown San Jose. That plant was at least ten feet tall and wide. It was in bloom all year round.

Sadly, an unknowing caretaker hacked Niles Cochet right down to the ground. The plant lingered for a few years, then died. How sad.

There was a time wherein I attempted to educate the perpetrators of such horticultural crimes. I don't do that, anymore. Folks sometimes whack rose plants with evangelistic fervor. They believe that the forces of righteousness are on their side. They believe that they are pruning roses the *right* way—if they think at all. That kind of person doesn't want to hear that his or her pruning "masterpiece" is a botanical horror show.

Nowadays, I just hope that hacked plants will receive adequate quantities of water and fertilizer during the growing season. Mostly though,

I pray that roses that have been damaged by pruning will survive to see better days.

Learn about the roses that you're going to prune

In my fifty-five-year career as a professional gardener and grower, I have communicated with uncounted thousands of accidental rose growers. That type of person moved into a property that had preexisting rose plants growing in the yard. Most of the accidental rose growers whom I have met were befuddled by the usually overgrown rose plants that they "inherited."

If you have fallen into that group, I advise you to proceed with caution. Unless you are an experienced rose grower, it is best to assume that you don't know what type of care and pruning your newly accumulated roses require.

Walk around the neighborhood and see what everyone else is growing. Chances are that the roses in other local gardens will look like those that are growing in *your* new garden.

Ask neighbors how they prune their roses. Ask several neighbors how they prune their roses. In this fashion, you can begin to build some sort of a consensus, if only in your own mind.

Contact rose societies in your area. They can provide you with tips on pruning roses. For the price of a small donation to their rose society, you might find a rose-society member who will help you prune your roses. Studying with an expert is a good way to learn any craft.

Caution! There are as many rose-pruning methods as there are people who prune roses! Find a knowledgeable rosarian who understands the pruning technique best suited to your rose-growing goals.

Joe and Jane natural, part one

I already mentioned the people who like to whack a rose back to stubs, so that they can win a prize. That kind of advice could be dangerous to your newly acquired rose plants.

But wait, kids, more confusion is on the way! The whack-'em-low rose folks have direct opposites: the don't-touch-my-plants crowd. Yes, that's right. Some folks who grow old garden roses don't believe roses should be pruned. That mind-set frequently results in a garden of Victorian decadence for about five to ten years.

At some point, unpruned rose plants begin to look like the brambles around Sleeping Beauty's castle. No one can get through the side gate. This sometimes creates a sad princess.

Somewhere between the two extremes of rose-pruning philosophy, there is a modality that is the best for you and your plants.

PRUNING EQUALS REPLACING

Did you know rose plants can live for hundreds of years? That longevity is made possible by an amazing trait; roses replace their worn-out parts with brand new canes. Old plants transform into new. If only humans shared the same trait. Wouldn't it be wonderful if you could grow a new leg to replace a painful knee?

Rose plants *can* live a very long time. But there's a trick; most plants will require assistance from their caretakers to accomplish that feat. Much of this help will be provided in the form of water and fertilizer.

Pruning is the *real* key to plant longevity. Rose plants *must* be pruned in a way that encourages cane replacement. But how do you prune for cane replacement? What do you cut, and what do you leave? Read on so that you can learn how rose plants grow. Rose pruning will be demystified, after you have attained that knowledge.

Geography and Weather Will Indicate
How You Should Prune Roses

● ● ●

Weatherman
Weatherman
Where are you?
Can you tell the truth?

Of storms
And floods
And frosty gales
I need to plan my day.

Do the plants require winter protection?
The combination of climate and relative plant hardiness will determine what type of plants can be safely grown outdoors in your area. Smart growers know that they can push the envelope a little. They cover their roses to protect them from the ravages of cold or variable weather.

Determine if the types of roses that are growing in your garden need to be winter protected. That information will provide you with a starting point for your specific rose-pruning job.

PRUNING WINTER-PROTECTED ROSES

Prune at the right time. Don't over prune the plants. Provide the plants with adequate water and fertilizer throughout the growing season. Seek local advice for specific information about winter protecting rose plants. That's my primary advice for people who live in cold climates.

Otherwise, please read on. I'm going to tell you how roses grow and age. No matter where you live, this information will help you and your roses.

PRUNING ROSE PLANTS THAT DO *NOT* NEED TO BE WINTER PROTECTED

Growers in warm climates are quite fortunate; they don't need to "butcher" their plants to facilitate winter-protection measures. Warm-climate pruning can be accomplished in a manner that is tailored to suit the plants.

Learn how your rose plants grow, so that you can understand their specific needs. Watch others prune, so that you can learn from their successes and failures.

The Most Important Rose-Pruning Concept

● ● ●

Little toes,
And button noses
Children are so dear.

But know you all,
Before they fall,
Babies grow away.

STAGE ONE

ROSES ARE GROWN FROM SEEDS or cuttings. Those are small things. But the plants don't stay small for long. Most well-grown rose plants soon begin to grow explosively. A two-inch, barely rooted cutting can easily become a three-foot plant in just a few weeks. This growth spurt is called the logarithmic growth stage. The plants are growing in a semi logarithmic fashion.

A newly grown rose plant's growth is produced in a small area, right down at ground level. I call that area "the zone of active growth."

STAGE TWO

Once their initial growth stage is over, most rose plants change. They don't want to remain ground-hugging bushes. They want to grow up. Roses are genetically programmed to become tall, rangy shrubs.

In the wild, roses generally produce one set of new canes each year. Those canes might not be long enough to reach up and above surrounding plants. Roses developed an interesting adaptation for overcoming "the curse of short canes"—they build scaffolds. Scaffolds are wonderful devices. Home builders and peach trees use them to carry weight.

Plants build scaffolds by growing new shoots on top of the old ones. Roses are quite adept at building themselves up. Scaffold building is great when roses need to grow out of a shrubby understory of wild plants. But that growing-out part isn't always acceptable in a garden situation. People might love a plant when it grows as a three-foot mound. But they might not be happy when it morphs into a five- or six-foot bramble.

A plant that overgrows its place is not always welcome. A tall, grown plant can interrupt important garden views. Large plants can also become serious safety hazards. Garden safety trumps all other considerations.

I have seen countless rose plants meet their end because they outgrew their homes. How sad for the plant.

JOE AND JANE NATURAL, PART TWO

Some of you are thinking in a different way, at this point. Many gardeners love their unpruned, overgrown roses. Hey, I concede this point; some unpruned rose plants are sumptuous. Many of them drip with blooms.

In a purely moral sense, one person doesn't have the right to judge the height of another person's rose bush. But such concepts can be horticulturally wrong for the plants.

Desired plant height can be something of an emotional issue. Grow your plants at a height that you and your plants find to be mutually agreeable.

Beyond plant height, there is a more important issue—plant health. Overgrown rose plants are dangerous to their own health and longevity.

THE EYES HAVE IT

All rose plants grow from a structure that is variously called a "bud" or an "eye." When they are young, roses have lots of dormant (sleeping) eyes at the very bottom of the plant (in their initial zone of active growth). Those eyes are waiting for a chance to break (grow). See "bud" in the glossary of terms.

But most roses aren't genetically programmed to produce new growth from the bottom of the plant. They build new canes on top of the old ones. Remember, roses are driven by millions of years of programming. It is telling them to grow up and out.

Over time, the old canes age and become vulnerable to overuse; and unbroken eyes that remain in the original zone of active growth age do, too. They eventually cease to be viable candidates for producing new growth.

This is the great power struggle that lies between a rose plant and its own dormant eyes. The plant's prime mandate is to reach up for the sun. It can best accomplish that task by growing from its upper buds, not the lower ones. The plant will favor the upper buds with nutrient fluids and growth hormones. The lower buds will not be favored. It will be stranded, down below.

Most unbroken eyes will break only if they are given human assistance. Lacking that help, very few (if any) of an overgrown rose plant's dormant eyes will ever break. At some point, unbroken eyes harden and become covered with a thick layer of bark. From that point onward, it is almost impossible for them to break.

Because the remaining lower eyes have been rendered into a state wherein they cannot break, they are said to be blind. Blind people cannot see. Blind canes have no eyes with which to produce new growth.

When a rose plant ceases to produce new canes, it is forced to rely upon its old ones. Some rose varieties have canes that don't age well. With time, they lose vigor or die. If all the canes die, the plant generally dies, too. That is how plants are lost.

Rose plants that stand upon hoary white legs are vulnerable things! Their future rests on stove wood piles.

HOW TO MAINTAIN A ROSE PLANT'S ORIGINAL ZONE OF ACTIVE GROWTH

Rose plants want to grow up. It is better for most of them to stay down. In that regard, roses have much in common with dogs. Gardeners and dog owners must decide how their charges will behave. Puppies and new rose plants are easy to train. That training is accomplished by teaching the caretakers.

If young rose plants are provided with adequate sunlight, water, and fertilizer, they will usually thrive. Young, vigorously growing rose plants should produce new canes from the original zone of active growth, down at ground level. That's great.

But we must remember most rose plants don't want to live as low-growing shrubs. Millions of years of evolution have programmed rose plants to find ways in which to dominate the local understory—your understory.

Many modern roses begin their march to garden domination in a casual way. They force second-generation breaks a few inches above the original zone of active growth. Some rose aggressors are not that subtle. They will sprout new breaks a few *feet* above their original zone of active growth.

Look at a few rose plants that are about three or four years old. You will probably see that the plants are comprised of a mixture of old and new canes. You also might notice that some of the newer canes built themselves on top of the older ones. Such plants have raised their zones of active growth to higher levels.

Gardeners should learn to recognize when a plant has raised its zone of active growth. At pruning time, they can put that knowledge to work.

Look for canes that have emerged below older ones. When you prune, leave the lowest-lying strong growth. If there are plenty of new canes, cut out others that have raised their zone of active growth.

I like to tell people, "Go down on your plants." This means that you should *always* look for opportunities to prune down on an existing cane. Note the location of a desirable cane. Make the pruning cut three inches above the desirable cane. Most rose varieties will respond to this type of knowledgeable pruning. It creates long-lived, well-mannered plants. See the "Long Stubs Are Ugly but Beneficial" chapter in this book.

Smart puppy owners don't allow their charges to jump up on human beings. Smart rose growers don't allow their plants to jump their canes on top of each other.

SOME TIPS FOR LOWERING THE ZONE OF ACTIVE GROWTH ON OVERGROWN ROSE PLANTS

I define a rose plant as being overgrown when its zone of active growth has migrated to a point that is six inches or more above the ground. Some folks might believe that is a rigid definition. It's not rigid at all. A rose that has raised its zone of active growth by just six inches is already beginning to go blind in its lower parts. If a given plant's zone of active growth soars up a foot or more, it's lower parts *will* go blind.

Some gardeners eventually notice that their rose plants aren't producing new basal breaks from the original zone of active growth. In many cases, it is too late reverse the damage. This is how plants decline and die.

But worry not, gentle gardener, all is not lost. You might not be able to restore a given plant's original zone of active growth. But you *can* recreate a plant in a healthier, more restrained form. In short, most overgrown rose plants can be improved with time, decent pruning, water, and fertilizer.

The key to lowering a plant's zone of active growth is to always prune down (if you safely can). Seek out vigorous lower growth and cut off what stands above.

Pruning is a type of surgery. When we prune roses, we cut or remove many of their various parts. This massed cutting usually occurs during just one session. Your plant is being subjected to several different surgical procedures, all at one go.

Treat overgrown plants with compassion. Don't prune them too much, the first time around. Let the plants recover from your ministrations. They will tell you how they want to grow, if you take the time to observe and learn.

The Second-Most Important Rose-Pruning Concept

● ● ●

Funny names;
The past in words
Dead languages,
In brief.
Of Bodkins,
Teasels,
And
Taps-to;
Whatever's lost is gone.

TAKE A CLOSE LOOK AT the canes that are produced by most bush-type rose plants. You might note that the canes are relatively thick at the bottom. About half or three-quarters of the way up a typical cane, the growth usually becomes slimmer.

The thin, upper portion arcs away from the main cane in a gentle curve. From the side, that arc looks like a dog's rear leg. Someone somewhere named the point where rose canes break and curve away the dogleg.

I believe that the knowledge of how rose-cane doglegs function is the second-most important rose-pruning concept. Why? It all comes down to how roses evolved. Wild roses live in a harsh, competitive world. They are surrounded by plants that attempt to grow up and steal the sun.

Uncounted species of insects, birds, and mammals eat various portions of rose anatomy.

Young rose shoots taste like candy to browsing animals. Some plants will not thrive when their tender parts are regularly trimmed. Not the noble rose! Roses were designed to have their top shoots browsed (or pruned). Rose plants can survive if the new top growth of their canes is damaged by frost or browsing animals. This is because rose plants generally have more dormant growth buds waiting to sprout, down on their lower canes.

Some rose types find it difficult to sprout if their lower canes are damaged. In response, roses developed tough lower canes. Most importantly, roses covered their canes with prickles (thorns). In so doing, the rose sent a message to the cold, cruel world: "Hey, guys, I can survive if you eat my tops, but not if you eat my canes. I will cover my important parts with thorns to make them unpalatable."

The critical portions of rose anatomy are located below the dogleg. Those portions were designed to be the scaffold and genetic repository of future growth. They were *not* designed to be turned into low, bare stumps.

If we take the time to notice, rose canes will demonstrate that fact. Look at the upper end of a rose cane that has been cut below the dogleg. You will see that it looks like the side view of a doughnut. The lower portions of rose canes have a ring of hard wood on the outside. Inside is a rounded area that is filled with a spongy material that is called "pith." Pith is *very* soft.

ROSE CANES ARE LIKE EGGSHELLS

Rose canes and eggshells have much in common. Both are hard, lightweight structures that are exceptionally strong and durable—until they are cracked. If you crack an egg, you will get an immediate, messy result. A cane crack that is made by pruning might not be visible. That kind of damage can take months to become apparent.

Rose canes don't always crack when they are cut below the dogleg. But the pith that lies at the center of the cane *will* always be exposed by such cuts. That is never good, in my opinion. Nature did *not* intend for soft, inner portions of rose canes to be exposed to the elements.

Yes, I know; rose canes that are cut below the dogleg will thrive. But in most cases, the cane will grow better if the dogleg portion is *not* removed. Some roses don't care if you cut them below the dogleg. Some roses *need* to be mowed to the ground each winter.

The trick lies in knowing which roses like to be mowed and which like to be pruned above the dogleg.

YOUR ROSES ARE ROTTEN

"Foetid" is a strange word. It is a variant of "fetid." Fetid things produce offensive odors. Rotting things give off fetid smells. People are surprised when they learn that there is a rotten rose. *Rosa foetida* was hung with that moniker due to the smell of her blooms. They *do* have a strange, musky odor.

Yellow and orange are new colors in the pallet of the genus *Rosa*. So are the modern lavender and coffee tones. Those colors were supplied via an infusion of genes from *Rosa foetida*. If you like brightly colored roses with shiny foliage, you can thank *Rosa foetida*. That rose also brought black spot susceptibility into modern roses.

WHY IS *ROSA FOETIDA* IMPORTANT TO PRESENT-DAY GARDENERS?

We live in a fast-changing world. Many things that provided foundations for change have been completely forgotten. Most people don't know that repeat-blooming yellow roses have only existed since the latter part of the nineteenth century. That might seem to be ancient history to a lot of people. But that's just a blink of the eye to the *Rosa foetida* descendants in your garden.

Rosa foetida has very soft canes. They split easily when they are cut. The canes then suffer grievously. This soft-cane trait was passed on to

Rosa foetida's ancestors, along with the bright colors. There is never something gained, but something else is lost, folks.

GREY PEARL LIVES

Repeat-blooming lavender-colored roses are new things. They all descended from a 1945 hybrid tea: Grey Pearl. The parents of Grey Pearl are only a few generations removed from their ancestor, *Rosa foetida*.

Grey Pearl was not a commercial success. The color was shocking to contemporary sensibilities. During the 1950s and 1960s, lavender roses were commonly associated with death. To the eyes of the day, lavender-colored roses had the pallid tone of corpses.

Some people in 1945 thought that lavender roses were quite interesting. But Grey Pearl didn't find much of a following. Why? The term "weak grower" might have been coined for Grey Pearl. The plants grew small in nursery fields. Nurseries soon discovered that bare-root plants Grey Pearl suffered grievously when they were not stored in exactly the right way.

Home gardeners found Grey Pearl to be impossible to grow. People who cut a long-stemmed flower of Grey Pearl reacted in horror as the whole cane died below the cut. (She is a foetida, all the way.) Hard 1950s-style pruning techniques finished off the variety.

Plant breeders were not dissuaded by contemporary color fads or by the weak growth habit of Grey Pearl. They saw great possibilities in this strange, new variety. They pounced on her genes with gusto.

The world saw Grey Pearl as an *ugly duckling*. Her descendants are swans. Sterling Silver came first and then the sublime Angel Face. Eventually came Lagerfeld, and all that passed beyond.

For those of us who lived in a world that saw few lavender roses, this is an amazing eventuality! We now have wonderfully fragrant, lavender-colored roses as far as the eye can see!

Ah, Grey peal's bad traits were behind left in the 1950s. The soft canes of *Rosa foetida* were infused into modern roses via Grey Pearl. Many Grey

Pearl descendants have retained her dislike of pruning techniques that cut below the dogleg.

Modern lavender roses do not possess the same weak habit as some of their ancestors. Most modern lavender varieties like to *grow*. Site rose varieties that make large plants in large places. Don't prune a large plant to make it fit into a small space. This is *especially* true of roses that are descended from *Rosa foetida*.

THE MOST IMPORTANT ACCOMPLISHMENT IN ROSE HISTORY CAN CREATE PRUNING PROBLEMS FOR YOU

In the late eighteenth century, roses from China were imported to Europe. Western minds named these new arrivals the Chinas and Teas. The new Chinese roses bloomed repeatedly. That trait alone was enough to make gardeners drool.

Contemporary growers soon discovered that some of the new Chinese roses had marvelous, high-centered blooms. That was quite a change from the carnation-like blooms of the old European roses.

European breeders quickly used the Chinas and Teas as breeding stock. New varieties were quickly introduced that exhibited the best traits of European and Chinese roses. They changed the world of flowers and gardening.

Doesn't it seem there is always a fly in the ointment? The Chinese roses gave much to the genus *Rosa*. But they also infused modern roses with a potential flaw; a tropical nature. Most modern roses aren't as cold hardy as their old European counterparts.

Roses received their infusion of Chinese genes less than 220 years ago. That period represents an eye blink in the long chain of plant evolution. Modern roses are plants that are much changed to the eye, but less so in their nature. Most repeat-blooming modern roses are Chinese at heart. They grow and bloom continuously. This part can create pruning challenges for modern gardeners.

Freezing temperatures occur in most of the places where people grow roses. In some areas, roses need to be pruned for winter protection. Roses are generally pruned low, to facilitate that procedure. Some modern, nearly Chinese varieties don't like to be cut below the dogleg.

Growers in mild climates have their own problems with modern hybrids. Many people don't want their plants to attain jungle-like proportions.

THE BOTTOM LINE

Roses need to be pruned. Rose lovers need to become proficient rose pruners. Much of that proficiency will be realized after you have attained the knowledge of two critical details about rose physiology; the zone of active growth and the rose cane dogleg.

Anyone who wants to become a truly proficient rose pruner *must* understand the appearance and function of doglegs. It is not a difficult concept. Take a good look at the canes of bush-type rose plants. It will become apparent to you. Once you understand the rose can dogleg concept, you are ready to begin pruning in an educated fashion.

The Mystery of the All-Mighty Basal Break

● ● ●

Mighty growth,
From the land
It comes from whence unknown.

Learn to love
Your Mother Earth
Thus, mysteries revealed.

NOT ALL ROSE VARIETIES CONTINUE TO PRODUCE NEW BASAL BREAKS

NOT ALL ROSE VARIETIES CONTINUE to produce new basal breaks after the initial log stage of growth is complete. Some rose varieties, like Angel Face, will fool you. They produce lots of basal breaks when they are young. When they get just a little older, they sometimes stop producing new basal breaks.

Caretakers must exercise great caution when they prune their roses for the first time. They must not assume that the plants will continue to be vigorous in the future. Proceed cautiously until you understand the long-term growth habits of your plants.

Some rose plants can thrive for decades after they have produced their last basal break. Their remaining canes should never *be removed*.

SOME VARIETIES ARE "PERPETUAL MOTION MACHINES"

Double Delight is the poster child for rose varieties that replace their old canes. Plants of Double Delight that receive adequate water, fertilizer, and pruning will generally replace *all* their canes every two years.

Somewhere between Duet (which almost never produces a new cane) and Double Delight (which almost always produces new canes), there is a wide, grey area. This is the place in which most rose types reside, in terms of how frequently they produce new basal breaks.

You can usually "persuade" most rose varieties to produce new basal breaks. That feat is accomplished by providing the plants with knowledgeable pruning.

Exhausted-Node Syndrome

● ● ●

Five o' clock
Gotta' get up
Gotta' lotta' work to do.

An' I ain't a bit lazy,
I ain't no kind of slacker,
I'm from a busy clan.

The work don't scare me,
The boss don't faze me,
The wife does what she has to do.

But I'll tell ya' now people-
I'm a little scared
I got a little problem to face.

You see, I'm a turnin' fifty,
It's early in the mornin',
An' I'm still tired from yesterday.
Scotch-Irish Melody.

NODES

LOOK AT A ROSE STEM. You will generally see that leaves emerge at regular intervals along the stem. The places where leaves emerge from stems are called "nodes." Most nodes contain at least one growth bud. Buds contain undifferentiated growth cells. Undifferentiated cells possess the ability to develop into roots or stems. All new growth in rose plants originates from an eye of one form or another.

Some of the eyes that lie at the base of the nodes never break (sprout). Other nodes become hotbeds of new growth. Over time, bud after bud will break from the same node.

But there is a limit to how much growth even the most active node can produce and sustain. At some point, a node that has previously produced an abundance of high-quality growth will slow down. Any new growth that the node produces will be weak. I call this condition "exhausted-node syndrome."

From a distance, exhausted nodes might appear to be healthy—but they aren't. It is not good for so much growth to be concentrated in a small area. It can lead to problems. Insects and fungi love crowded conditions.

It gets worse from there. As the number of dormant eyes in a node break, fewer of them remain available to grow in the future. The stronger eyes in a node generally break first. When they are exhausted, weaker eyes sprout. This can lead to a loss of vigor in the canes that grow from exhausted nodes.

Rose plants are like people; they can become creatures of habit. Some canes produce their growth from just one node. When that node *finally* stops producing new growth, the whole cane will suffer. If that is the best or only cane on a plant, it will suffer grievously.

PRUNING PLANTS THAT HAVE EXHAUSTED NODES

Proceed cautiously when you prune plants that suffer from exhausted-node syndrome. Examine the entire plant. Note the condition of its other canes.

Do they contain exhausted nodes? How much strong, new growth is on the plant?

Here's the most important question of all: Is strong growth emerging from any point below an exhausted node? If the answer to that question is yes, there's an easy solution; cut off the exhausted node, and leave the growth that stands below. If strong, new growth is *not* emerging below an exhausted node, proceed cautiously.

Give a plant that suffers from exhausted-node syndrome plenty of water and fertilizer. Many tired old plants can be reinvigorated with care. Reinvigorated plants will sometimes initiate vigorous new growth below an exhausted node. When that happens, you can safely cut above the new growth and remove the exhausted node.

Climbing rose varieties commonly have very long canes. It is easy to detect exhausted-node syndrome on that type of cane. But smaller plants get exhausted-node syndrome, too. Smart growers know that the best treatment for node exhaustion is prevention. Grow your plants in ways that achieve and maintain low levels of active growth. Remove nodes before they become exhausted.

Tread Softly with the Old

• • •

Lovely rose
In a vase.
Its visage now divine.

But week-old roses
Are a passing sort,
Enjoy them while you can.

PEOPLE, DOGS, AND ROSE PLANTS tend toward fragility, as they age. Looks can be deceiving. Some individuals may outwardly appear to be vigorous—but they are still old.

An inexperienced pruner might see a ten-foot tangled mass of rose canes and think: "This is a vigorous plant. I'm going to cut it hard. It will grow back, good as new." Most people can't see through their own haste and inexperience. They are unable to conceptualize that it might have taken fifty years for a bush-type rose plant to become a tangled, ten-foot bramble. They might not know that most of the new growth is emerging from the very top of the plant.

Pruners also might not realize that they are dealing with a delicate type of rose. Some roses resent harsh pruning—*especially* when they have become overgrown.

Time is the antidote for dealing with old, overgrown rose plants. Gentleness is the medicine. Proceed slowly with your pruning efforts.

Five-year plans

It generally takes an experienced pruner about three to five years to successfully reduce an overgrown rose plant. It is dangerous and risky to attempt a rose-plant-reduction program in less time.

The first stage in a rose-plant-reduction program is realization. Responsible parties must be aware that plant restoration will take a long time. They must then have the patience to allow the job to proceed over its allotted period of years. No abbreviation of the schedule can occur. This is a botanical contract between the responsible party, the pruner, and the plant.

How to prune an overgrown rose plant

Pruning overgrown rose plants does not involve a bunch of complicated processes. The rules are simple. Don't cut very much the first year. Provide plenty of water and fertilizer during the following growing season. Sit back and wait. The roses will tell you what to do from there.

After a light, first year pruning, most overgrown rose plants will initiate strong growth from lower points on their canes. Such new growth will generally not emerge from the very bottom of the plant. But strong new growth will usually emerge from lower points on the existing canes, than the previous year. That's the important part; the zone of active growth should be on its way down.

The second year of a remedial pruning program will reveal the first fruits of your labor. That reward is represented in the form of strong growth that is emerging from lower points on the canes. Thus, the harvest is made.

Year three generally should generally be a repeat of its predecessors. Don't prune too much. Cut above strong, low growth. Keep the water and fertilizer coming.

Many truths will be revealed during the fourth year of a remedial pruning scheme. Some growers will note that their plants have reached an improvement plateau. Fourth-year plateau plants generally have more vigor and health than they did way back at the beginning of the program. But many of them will *not* relocate their zones of active growth to lower positions.

No significant new growth will emerge from the lower portions of plateau plants. Most of that type will never produce new basal breaks from their lower portions.

Stabilization and maintenance are the future watchwords for overgrown plants that have reached an improvement plateau. Preserve and protect their existing canes. Don't prune too much from the actively growing portions of the plant (if any). Give the plants adequate water and fertilizer.

Hope for the best, but plan for the worst with overgrown plants that don't improve. Who knows? Maybe a plant miracle will happen; new growth might emerge from a lower level.

Year five in a remedial pruning program is a milestone. It marks the nominal end of an overgrown-plant-reduction program. That sounds wonderful—and final. But rose plants are living things, not bags of cement. We can't manufacture rose plants in accordance with anyone's five-year plan.

The fifth remedial pruning will usually reveal that all overgrown plants have reached a plateau of one sort or another. Remember, you are dealing with older rose plants, not just-planted "babies."

By year five, some formerly overgrown plants will be superstars. Most of their old, original canes will have been replaced by new ones. Plants in this category have greatly reduced zones of active growth.

I find it quite gratifying to look at a plant that has been improved by a plant-reduction program. My joy arises from a simple aspect: both the plant and its caretaker have won. The Buddhist part of me knows such things rarely occur.

Until then, you should be happy with the results that you have already received. It is imperative that you protect a plateau plant's existing canes; its future rests on stove wood piles.

How to protect stove wood canes
Support from a friend

Very old rose canes *do* look at lot like pieces of firewood. They are grey-brown, gnarly old things. They gained their wizened appearance by living for a long time. Canes of that type sometimes live for a *very* long time. They just need some help from *you*. Overgrown rose plants some-times require artificial support to remain upright. Please read the "Tying Roses Is Serious Business" chapter of this book. It will tell you how to support old canes.

Sunscreen and insect repellent

Despite my best efforts to the contrary, some of the rose plants in my gar-den have very old canes. I paint old canes. This reflects heat and helps to keep the cane cool. It also repels insects. Paint will help some rose canes to live indefinitely.

Please read the "Painting and Sealing" chapter in this book. It will tell you how to paint rose canes.

Caution! Only use paint that has been formulated for horticultural uses! Other types contain chemicals that can harm plants!

Caution! Do not use black-colored or asphalt-containing products to seal cuts or to paint canes! These products will cause the temperature of painted cuts to rise. This inhibits healing and plant growth.

Pruning Rose Plants That Are Still Producing New Basal Breaks from the very Bottom of the Plant

● ● ●

New kid on the block
An old tale told-
Anew.

New kid play with me today!
Your perfect life
A charm.

Assess first

Pruning is preceded by assessment. Look at a plant, and determine how it grew during the past season.

If a plant received plenty of sunlight, water, and fertilizer, it should possess a good mix of new and older basal breaks

An introduction to rose-plant mathematics
Math lesson number one

The peach is a member of the greater Rose family. I have heard many old timers say that untrained amateurs should never remove more than 25 percent of an average peach tree's new growth. That portion is generally sufficient to thin the tree, but not enough to cause lasting damage.

The 25 percent removal percentage works well with many roses, too. Using that formula, a rose plant that is four feet tall and wide should be reduced to three feet, all around.

MATH LESSON NUMBER TWO

Let's do some basic rose-plant arithmetic: plant A has eight canes that originate at ground level. In this example, four of the canes are less than two years old. The remainder are somewhat older.

I would remove two of the oldest canes and leave all that are of a more recent vintage. In the above example, I recommended that just two out of eight canes should be removed (25 percent). That is the highest percentage of canes that I will normally remove from a rose plant in a single year. Harsher pruning might shock the plant.

In a perfect world, one or more basal breaks would be removed from a given plant, each year. Sadly, we don't live in a perfect world; proceed with care.

Caution! If a plant isn't producing new canes, don't remove any old ones!

Every rose plant and variety has its own optimal pruning percentage. Diligence and experience will teach you how to determine these percentages in the roses that you prune.

Proceed slowly, until you learn.

ROSE MATH PUT TO WORK

Before you begin to prune a given rose plant, ask some questions: How high above ground level is the zone of active growth? How many canes does the plant possess? How many of them have doglegs? How many of the canes are new? How many canes suffer from exhausted-node syndrome?

The answers to these questions will define your plant—and how you should accomplish the pruning process.

It is imperative you understand the age and role of each type of cane a given rose plant possesses. After you acquire that understanding, you will be mentally equipped to do a decent pruning job.

Belle of Portugal, Charlotte Armstrong, Mermaid, *Rosa chinensis* "Mutabilis," *Rosa roxburghii*, and Susan Louise all share a wonderful characteristic: they have canes that age well.

I have seen rose canes of the above-listed varieties that were thicker than a man's waist. Such canes generally have the deeply furrowed bark of oak firewood. Long-lived canes are a desirable trait for a plant that will receive minimal pruning. The will carry the plant into the future.

Altissimo, Double Delight, and Sombreuil all share a different characteristic: the members of this group have canes that age quickly and lose vigor. Varieties that have short-lived canes don't build reliable scaffolds. They must be pruned for cane replacement.

An Assortment of Rose-Pruning Concepts

● ● ●

Jumbled box
Of cast-off things
Reminders from the past.
Too precious for the junkman's heap.
Lost for years on end.

THE RIGHTS OF PEOPLE *ALWAYS* TRUMP THE RIGHTS OF ROSES

THE FIRST AND LAST JOB of all growers is to ensure the safety of the people who pass through their gardens. Don't forget how much damage rose thorns can do to humans and other animals. No rose plant should be allowed to become a garden hazard.

WAS THE PLANT PRUNED LAST YEAR?

For pruning purposes, all rose plants fall into two categories: those that were pruned last year and those that were not.

If a rose plant was pruned last year, note if the task was accomplished in a competent manner. If the plant was pruned reasonably well, follow that same pattern in the future.

If the plant produced new basal breaks during the previous growing season, remove an appropriate quantity of old canes. Be sure to follow the cane-removal guidelines I have written elsewhere in this book.

If the plant was *not* pruned last year, proceed cautiously. Such plants should be considered as being overgrown. Read the "Proceed Cautiously with the Old" chapter in this book. It will guide you through the process of pruning overgrown pants.

Pruning with a chaser

For me, remedial pruning jobs require a good deal of forethought and agreement. The forethought takes place in my own head. The agreement comes from a plant's responsible party. That person needs to agree to a five-year plant-reduction program. The responsible party also needs to promise that the plants will receive adequate water and fertilizer in the coming growing seasons.

That is a large commitment for anyone to make. But it is the best way to reduce an overgrown plant.

Don't prune plants that won't receive irrigation

People sometimes ask me to prune unirrigated roses. I usually refuse their requests. I like to help people, but I usually defer for the health of the plant.

Rose plants need water to grow and recover from the stress of being pruned. An unirrigated plant might not have the energy to replace the growth that has been removed.

Pruning creates wounds. Wounds are healed by active plant growth. That requires energy. Plants that are stressed for lack of water and fertilizer don't create much energy. Stressed plants have difficulty healing the wounds that are created by normal pruning.

I know there are exceptions to my "don't prune unirrigated plants" rule. But in my experience, those exceptions are few and far between. Exercise great caution if you *must* prune unirrigated rose plants. Don't attempt such a job, if you are not an experienced rose pruner.

Some plants are better off when they are left unpruned.

Cut and remove

Here's a plant safety tip; when you prune rose plants, immediately remove the severed portions. A cut cane will sometimes fall deeper into the plant. If they fall to the ground, they assume the appearance of basal breaks. Anyone who prunes that plant will believe that the cut cane is a basal break. That will alter the mathematics of the pruning job. The pruner might think, "Wow! This plant has a lot of new basal breaks. I can remove these canes." They don't realize that one or more of their canes are cut pieces. I have made this error, folks—it's easy to do.

Remove *all* cut portions—-*immediately*

Don't allow rose canes to become saw blades!
Rose canes are like saw blades. They have teeth scattered around their circumference. It is quite tempting to cut a cane at the bottom and then pull it out of the plant. Don't do that! The prickles (thorns) of the canes will cut neighboring growth. Cut canes into several smaller pieces. You can then safely remove them without hurting the plant. It is especially important that you use this cane-removal method when you prune a plant from below.

Pruning to make a plant fit into a confined space
People sometimes ask me how to prune roses that have outgrown their allotted spaces. Unwanted size gains are sometimes the result of a lack of proper pruning. Those plants can generally be reduced with a long-term plant=reduction program.

Vigorous roses are sometimes planted in spaces that are too small. The inevitable reaction to this situation is to whack the poor rose into oblivion. Some rose varieties will meekly submit to such treatment; they will become abbreviated plants.

Other roses regard draconian pruning as an indication that more growth is required. They will grow even more.

I am an advocate for removing roses that have grown too large for a given space. Find another plant that will make a better neighbor. Hard pruning will *not* compensate for bad planning.

Hard pruning will *NOT* create bigger blooms

Leaves create the energy that plants need to live and grow. If you prune rose very hard, it will have fewer leaves. How is that supposed to create larger blooms?

By my personal definition, hard pruning generally means cutting below the dogleg. That will stress the plant even more—which might make it produce smaller blooms.

Tip every bit of growth

Cut the tips of all remaining growth, no matter how small. A tiny, one-inch blind bottom shoot can sometimes grow a mighty new cane—*if* it is tipped.

It's as much about cleaning as it is pruning

I regularly walk past a row of houses that has plants of Betty Boop growing in their front yards. That's the way it goes with plants. Folks sometimes plant what they see thriving in their neighbor's gardens.

Most of the Betty Boop plants in that row of gardens receive rudimentary winter pruning. The plants in front of one house do not.

The plants of Betty Boop that get pruned are relatively disease-free. Fifty feet away, unpruned plants of the same variety are covered with rust and mildew.

"Last year's leaves can cause this year's disease." I coined that phrase to be a teaching aid. It helps my students to remember that garden cleanup is a critical aspect of the rose-pruning process. Rose leaves are "savings accounts" for insects and disease. Remove the leaves from your plants in the autumn. Clean any weeds and debris that have accumulated below the plants. If you accomplish those small jobs, your garden will be a healthier place, next year.

Pruning saves money

Most rose varieties can renew themselves indefinitely. They require water, fertilizer, and pruning, to accomplish that botanical feat. It is not a difficult thing to do. Renew and reinvigorate your rose plants; don't rebuy them.

Long Stubs Are Ugly but Beneficial

● ● ●

Style,
Oh, style!
Let's chase awhile—
A passing fancy-free.
Let's treat our eyes
(And those of others),
To a little puff of steam.

LOOK AT PHOTOGRAPHS THAT DEMONSTRATE rose pruning. Many of them will have a close-up of what they call a "correct" cut. Every depiction of a pruned rose cane I ever have ever viewed had two things in common: the cut was at a forty-five-degree angle and originated about one-quarter to one-half inch above an eye. Everybody seems to know that is the right kind of pruning cut. The problem is everybody is *wrong*.

Growth buds line up along rose stems like beads on a string. Buds usually alternate around stems; they rarely form on opposite sides of each other. The side of the stem that is on the opposite of an eye is usually smooth and blank. The smooth and blank side of a stem is a nutrient "superhighway." It carries much of the stem's life-giving nutrient liquids.

When a stem is cut, so is the nutrient flow. The stem that was once a busy nutrient superhighway has suddenly become a quiet cul-de-sac. There is no "through traffic" of life-giving fluids.

Eyes are like the driveways that exit from cul-de-sacs. Nutrients flow into the "bud-eye driveways" from the lower portions of the plant.

But there is no nutrient driveway on the blank portion of the stem that lies behind the eye. It became a dead end when the top of the cane or stem was removed. Some nutrients will continue to flow to the blank rear portion of the cane. But the nutrient stream will not be delivered with the same force as before it was cut. The newly made dead end has become a dead zone, nutrient wise.

The portion of the stem that lies behind the eye is not technically dead. It has become something akin the dreaded dead zones that cell phone users encounter. There is not enough bandwidth (fluid pressure) to download large files (nutrients).

Any pruning cut is a bet. The pruner is wagering that strong, new growth will emerge from the eye that lies below a cut. When the eye grows explosively, the bet is won. Wounds are healed. The nutrient dead zone, which lies behind the bud, becomes engulfed by the tissues of a strong, new shoot.

But it doesn't always work that way. Some eyes grow slowly. When that happens, the flow of nutrient fluids to the dead zone slows down a little more. This further reduces the flow of nutrient fluid to both the bud eye and the dead zone. This vicious cycle sometimes results in weak growth or eye death.

Rose plants need to be pruned. But we *don't* have to create dead zones on the ends of rose canes! We can, instead, create nutrient turnarounds. We do that by leaving long stubs above the growth bud.

Long stubs leave more bark surface area on the cut portion of the cane that remains above an eye. Bark contains layers that transport nutrient fluids. I believe that the augmented bark area of a long stub increases the quantity of nutrient fluids that flow to the dead zone. This helps to keep the dead zone alive.

Eyes benefit from long stubs, too. Eyes thrive when they are backed by healthy dead zones.

Long stubs are "insurance" against bad pruning cuts. Bad cuts are ones that crack canes or tear the bark behind the eye. A bad cut, which occurs in conjunction with a typical quarter-inch-long stub, is almost always the guarantor of top-bud death. When that happens, the cane dies back to the next bud that lies below. The next bud in line is normally on the wrong side of the cane. A growth bud that is poorly positioned will generally produce a problem cane.

I seldom leave pruning stubs that are less than one inch long. When I cut very thick canes, I leave longer stubs.

For example; when I cut canes that are one inch thick, I leave a stub that is two or three inches long. If I cut a cane that is four inches thick, I leave a twelve-inch stub.

Long stubs leave a huge quantity of bark area and wood above an actively growing portion of a large cane. This allows the stub to safely die back above the growing portion.

Note: there is always a possibility that unseen and unwanted dormant eyes will break on a long stub that stands above a desirable eye. Pinch off any growth that subsequently breaks above desired eye.

I have been told numerous times that I am wrong for leaving long stubs on my roses. Most of the complaints seem to follow the logic that long stubs are ugly. I concede on that point: long stubs *are* ugly.

But I *won't* deny *the* truly important consideration; it is *always* better for the plant when long stubs are left above a desirable eye. Long stubs seldom die back enough to harm the eyes that lie beneath them.

FORTY-FIVE DEGREE CUTS ARE FINE FOR PICTURE FRAMES

What about the forty-five-degree cut of lore and legend? People use them because they look fast and stylish. In comparison, the plain ol' straight cut that I use on my cuts appears to be downright clunky.

But straight cuts are better. Why? Because the even edge of a straight cut will receive nourishment from the plant around its entire circumference.

When long stubs are a year or two old, I sometimes trim them. But I don't cut off very much (if at all). If the cane is growing vigorously, I generally leave well enough alone.

Paint your stubs

Paint any stub that is over half inch in diameter. This will promote healing. It will also reflect sunlight away from the dead zone that lies behind the growth bud.

Read the "Painting and Sealing" chapter of this book. It will tell you how to safely paint pruning stubs.

Caution! Only use paint that has been formulated for horticultural uses! Other types contain chemicals that can harm plants!

Caution! Do not use black-colored or asphalt-containing products to seal cuts or to paint canes! These products will cause the temperature of painted cuts to rise. This inhibits healing and plant growth.

Use Aseptic Technique

● ● ●

Dirt-bag,
Dirt bags
(All of us).
A putrid mass o' stink.
Our bodies made
Of primal things,
Which eat us when we die.

MOTHER EARTH IS POPULATED BY mobile things. People, plants, and diseases are always seeking new horizons, new places to colonize.

Most plants are infested with diseases and pests of one sort or another. Roses are no different. Many of them are infested with one or more viruses. Rose viruses vary in their effect and intensity. The effects of some viruses are barely noticeable. Others possess the ability to destroy the genus *Rosa*.

Spring dwarf is just one of several presently known viruses (or virus-like diseases) that could devastate roses in the future. Spring dwarf has a particularly nasty aspect: it may take several years for infested plants to become symptomatic (to show outward signs of the disease). Why is it that bad? Pruning shears accumulate biological products from the plants that they cut. If those biological products contain viruses, the tools contain viruses, too. A contaminated tool can infect the next plant that it cuts. Things can progress in this unhappy fashion for several years. By the time that good ol' Spring dwarf virus wakes up from its long sleep, a whole garden might be infected.

But wait, there's more! What about the plants that you pruned down at the park? What about the slip of Distant Drums that you gave to aunt Tilly in Buffalo? Guess what? Those plants also might have been infected by your contaminated tools.

Medical professionals use aseptic techniques. They use methods that decrease the possibility that microorganisms will be transmitted to or from patients and staff.

We live and garden in a dangerous world. We must use aseptic techniques in our gardens, fields, and nurseries. This will not eliminate the possibility that our plants will be contaminated with plant pathogens. But we *can* reduce the odds that our plants will be infected. In so doing, we can prevent catastrophe in our gardens (and in those of others).

I use 70 percent or 90 percent isopropyl (rubbing) alcohol to sterilize my shears. Some folks prefer other sterilizing agents. I believe that isopropyl alcohol is the best.

Sterilize every blade makes plant contact (including shovels and hoes). Sterilize your shears before you make the first cut of the day. Sterilize your shears when you move from one plant to another. Sterilize your shears when you finish work for the day.

Sterilize pruning shears by immersing them up to the adjustment nut in alcohol. Open and close the shears a few times. Wipe off the blade with a clean paper towel.

Sawzall, baby!

Reciprocating saws changed the world of pruning. They allow us to easily make clean cuts without damaging the plants. They also save wear and tear on the human body.

I have a box of spare reciprocating-saw blades. I use one blade for each plant that I prune. I place the used blades in an alcohol bath as soon as they are removed from the saw. I then scrub the soaked blades with a wire brush.

Caution! Spring dwarf is a pernicious disease! Destroy all plants, soil, and containers that contact plants that are infected with Spring dwarf! Do not attempt to grow another plant from the greater Rose family in a location that you know is infested with Spring dwarf!

How to Make Superior Pruning Cuts

● ● ●

Surgeon's cut.
Or bludgeon strike?
Which shall we use, today?

Cave-man's club,
Exchanged for knowledge.
A bargain made of dreams.

How to make good pruning cuts: part one

Good cuts are made by sharp shears of an appropriate type. Don't *ever* use anvil-type shears. They crush canes. Bypass shears are the best and only type of pruning shear.

Use hand shears to cut canes that are a half inch in diameter, or less. Use lopping shears to cut canes that are a half inch to one inch in diameter. Use a saw to cut canes that are over one inch in diameter.

Caution! Do not cut stems that are more than one-half inch in diameter with hand shears! The muscles and tendons of your hands are not intended for that kind of stress. Use lopping shears or pruning saws to cut stems that are larger than a half inch in diameter.

How to make good pruning cuts: part two

When I was just a kid, I regularly heard old timers ask the following rhetorical question: "How can you tell that someone is a professional fruit-tree pruner?" That question inevitably solicited the following response: "He's the guy who has a sharpening stone in his back pocket."

I sharpen my shears every day. When I am accomplishing large-scale pruning or deadheading jobs, I sharpen my shears three or four times a day.

How do I sharpen my shears? I'm not going to tell you! Why not? Because shear sharpening is a *very* dangerous activity. I don't want to assume liability by telling you how to accomplish a dangerous task. You're going to have to figure out how to get it done yourself. Seek a professional shear sharpener.

Lubricate pruning shears before you begin work. Lubricate shears after two hours of use. It will extend the life of the tool. The shears will also be easier to operate.

How to make good pruning cuts: part three

Make pruning cuts with a fast, sure motion. Not too fast, or accuracy of cut will be lost. Not too slow, lest the cane be crushed, rather than cut.

Practice pruning cuts on trash-plant species and brush that has been removed from rose plants.

How to make good pruning cuts: part four

Pruning saws don't receive much credit. But when it comes to removing large stubs or canes, no other tool will get the job done.

I was raised in the era when saw cuts were made by hand. Using hand saws required a lot of skill. It was also a physically debilitating task. Hand saws still have their place in the modern rose pruner's tool box. Hand saws make wonderful, delicate cuts.

I seldom use hand saws for pruning. I have found a better way. Reciprocating saws changed the world of rose- and fruit-tree pruning. Those tools can make large, small, close, clean, and accurate cuts. Reciprocating saws reduce the strain on human muscle and sinew.

"Practice makes perfect" is the motto for using reciprocating saws. Practice on fallen limbs and broomsticks, if you will. Just practice.

Use blades that are designed specifically for plant pruning.

Caution! Exercise caution when using power equipment. Use an appropriate suite of safety equipment. Read the operator's manual for any power equipment that you operate.

Caution! Reciprocating-saw blades can spread disease from plant to plant! Use a reciprocating-saw blade on just one plant, and then soak the blade in a pan of 70 percent or 90 percent isopropyl (rubbing) alcohol. Use a wire brush to clean sawdust and sap from soaked blades.

Painting and Sealing

● ● ●

Stucco wall
Upon a lath.
The story old as time.

Upright sticks
Made smooth by hands,
To keep away the cold.

PRUNING CUTS ARE WOUNDS. MEDICAL professionals cover human wounds with bandages to facilitate the healing process. Large pruning cuts also need to be covered. The controversial question is, "How?"

I grew up during the waning days of asphalt-based pruning sealers. Farmers and gardeners alike believed that plant wounds and cuts would heal better when they were slathered with a thick, gloppy coat of asphalt paste.

We were all *wrong* in making that assumption. Why? It all comes down to enzymes. Enzymes facilitate important chemical reactions in plants and animals. They change chemicals into forms that are usable to living things. But enzymes have a problem: many of them are temperature specific. This means that they only work within a narrow temperature range.

Parents and medical professionals freak out when a child's body temperature approaches 104 degrees Fahrenheit. Why? Enzymes are one big reason. Some human enzymes stop functioning at about 104 degrees Fahrenheit. You can't live without enzymes. Neither can your rose plants. Rose enzymes are temperature specific, too. (Though the temperature range is not as narrow as it is with humans.)

The asphalt paste that we once slathered on plants is black. Black objects absorb heat. Black objects absorb heat become hotter than their lighter-colored surroundings. This means that black-painted rose wounds can be hotter than is ideal for proper enzymatic function. In operative terms this means that black-painted plant wounds might not heal rapidly. Cane dieback and death can result.

Latex-based paints ushered in a new era of plant wound sealing. Smart orchardists painted wounds and whole tree trunks with white latex paint. The clouds opened and choirs of angels began to sing for all who love plants. For a while, anyway. Then somebody got a brilliant idea, "Let's put fungicides into latex paints, so we can prevent black mold." Oh boy! Yesterday's beneficial plant sealant became today's potential plant *killer*.

Latex house paints joined asphalt-based sealers on the dangerous, do-not-use list (one man's opinion on *that* thought, folks).

Farwell products of Wenatchee, Washington, recognized the need for a plant sealer that is safe and effective. They developed a line of latex-based products that work well on roses and fruit trees. I have used many different Farwell sealing products. I prefer the compound they have named Doc Farwell's Seal and Heal. It is a green-colored, latex-based paint that is applied with a brush. On roses and fruit trees, I paint all cuts and stubs that are one inch in diameter or larger.

I believe that it is possible to transmit viruses from plant-to-plant via infected paint brushes. Avoid possible cross-contamination by decanting a tiny amount of Doc Farwell's Seal and Heal into a sterile dish. Apply the paint from one dish on one specific plant grouping or type.

I also use a fresh, sterilized paint brush each time that I paint a different plant grouping or variety.

I sterilize all paint brushes and paint decanters with 70 percent or 90 percent isopropyl alcohol.

Caution! Only use paint that has been formulated for horticultural uses! Other types contain chemicals that can harm plants!

Caution! Do not use black-colored or asphalt-containing products to seal cuts or to paint canes! These products will cause the temperature of painted cuts to rise. This inhibits healing and plant growth.

Pruning Hybrid Teas, Floribundas, and Grandifloras

● ● ●

Waldorf salad;
Made of apples,
Sometimes grapes,
(A few).
Flavors meld
Upon your palate
Changing while you chew.

FLORIBUNDAS AND GRANDIFLORAS HAVE BECOME de-facto hybrid teas, in my opinion. That is because most of the differences that once existed between the hybrid teas, floribundas, and grandifloras have gradually disappeared.

This melding of the classes occurred because floribundas and grandifloras were bred to produce hybrid tea-type blooms. That look is required to win prizes in formal competitions.

This chapter will cover a few general pruning guidelines for the de-facto hybrid teas. Even though the concepts in this chapter also apply to floribundas and grandifloras, I refer mostly to hybrid teas, beyond this point.

I'm certain that many experienced rosarians agree with me on these points. Class designations are meaningless to most gardeners. They only care how about the performance of the plants in their own gardens.

A big ol' class

Hybrid teas have been grown and bred for about 150 years. In that time, thousands upon thousands of varieties have been introduced.

There is a great deal of variation in the ways in which hybrid teas grow. Some produce canes that top out at about eighteen inches. Others produce canes that are six or eight feet tall. Many are vigorous basal-break machines. Others are very stingy with their new growth.

Even though hybrid teas grow in divergent ways, they also share many commonalities. For example, most hybrid teas grow best when their plants are entirely comprised of canes that are four years old, or less. That is a best-case objective. It will not be possible with some varieties. Some hybrid teas do not reliably produce new canes. Other varieties will produce new canes, *if* they are given excellent care.

Awareness is a byproduct of experience. Experience comes with practice. Practice will enable you to look at a strange plant and instantly comprehend the pertinent details of its makeup. When we can comprehend the fine points of a plant's growth habit, we can formulate a sound pruning strategy.

Pruning strategies should always include mathematical equations. Is the plant overgrown? By how much? How high is the zone of active growth? How many canes does the plant possess? What are the ages of the canes? How many new canes were produced during the previous growing season? Does the plant have any exhausted nodes? If so, how many? Does the plant require hard pruning to make it fit into the garden? How many hours of direct sunlight will a plant receive?

Factor in care. Will the plant receive adequate water and fertilizer throughout the next growing season? Will the plant receive supplemental, midseason pruning?

Now we come to the style points. Do you know if a given variety resents hard pruning? Will it replace the canes that are removed during pruning?

Once you have defined the basic arithmetic of a given plant, you can begin to prune. Don't remove more than 25 percent of the canes on *any* rose plant. If a plant didn't produce new canes in the previous year, don't remove *any* canes.

Don't cut below the dogleg.

Cut the tips of all remaining growth, no matter how small. A tiny one-inch blind bottom shoot can sometimes grow into a mighty new cane, *if* it is tipped.

If a plant must be hacked to make it fit into a given space, it is probably the wrong variety for a given usage.

Watch out for varietal differences. Even though some of the roses in your gardens are in the same class, they grow in different ways. Your plants are individuals, not perfect little matchsticks, lined up in a box. Look for the differences in your plants, and prune them accordingly.

Most hybrid teas, grandifloras, and floribundas are easy to grow and forgiving of mistakes, *if* you prune them well and provide them with adequate sunlight, water, and fertilizer.

Pruning a Mixture of Miniatures

● ● ●

Elfin kind
Are in our midst.
Too tiny to behold.

They hide in the shadows
Of modern times,
Lost now to our sight.

MUTTS

THANKS TO THE GREAT RALPH Moore and others of like mind, miniatures have been bred with just about every family of rose on earth. This has created a plethora of strange and unusual genetic mixtures. Many of those "mutts" possess gross differences in plant form and bloom type, but they have been lumped together in the miniature class.

Some of the varieties in this mixed-up class have special cultural and pruning requirements. This is yet another case wherein time and experience will provide you the knowledge that you need to grow and prune your charges.

JUST HOW MINI IS YOUR MINIATURE ROSE?

Some miniature roses top out at six inches. Others, such as Winter Magic and Magic Carrousel sometimes leap up three or four feet. That is quite a height difference for varieties that are ostensibly in the same class.

Miniature roses have been widely grown and bred for about eighty years. In that time, the blooms of the minis have gotten larger. The plants have grown in stature. Truth be told: most modern mini roses are anything *but* miniature. Those who prune miniature roses must be aware of how tall a given variety wants to grow.

Don't mercilessly cut a plant to make it qualify for the term "miniature." If a plant is too tall for a given spot, move it to where it can expand to its optimal height.

Well-grown miniature roses can sometimes be the queens of new basal breaks. Pruning that type of rose plant is generally fast and fun. There isn't much brainwork involved; remove the canes that are more than one year old.

Some miniature varieties, such as Sweet Chariot can be cut down to within an inch of the ground, each Winter. That job can be safely accomplished with pruning shears, hedge trimmers, or lawn mowers. Sweet Chariot and varieties of like kind will respond by producing vast quantities of new growth.

If your miniatures aren't producing many new canes, proceed with caution. Don't remove old canes from *any* rose plant that isn't producing new ones.

Provide slow-growing miniatures with adequate sunlight, water, and fertilizer. You might find that they explode with growth and blooms.

Pruning the Two Main Types of Climbing Roses

●　●　●

Names created by unknowing men,
Sitting in a room.
Well removed
From the garden's teaching,
It's all there if you look…

CLIMBERS DON'T CLIMB!

I DEFINE A "CLIMBER" AS being any rose plant that has been allowed to maintain a permanent height of six feet or more. That's a loose definition, but it's the best I can do.

Flawed as it might be, I believe that my idea of what constitutes a climbing rose is better than the official definition. That is an easy statement to make, because there truly isn't much in the way of an official definition of the terms "climber" or "climbing roses."

The climber designation comprises what is sometimes called a "lumper class." Lumper classes exist in many branches of science. They are always confused and controversial repositories of types.

Roses have been lumped into the climber class because they possess a signature similarity; they create canes that are longer than those that are normally expected on bush-type rose plants.

Don't look for deep botanical implications in the term climber, folks; they are truly nothing more than plus-sized rose plants.

FILL YOUR HEAD WITH KNOWLEDGE BEFORE YOU FILL YOUR HANDS WITH SHEARS

Climbers are more difficult to prune than bush-type roses. Part of that difficulty arises from the fact that climbing roses are generally larger than their bush counterparts. That side of the pruning dynamic is explained in the "Match climbers to your stature" section of this chapter.

Climbing rose plants can be complex things. They generally contain a mixture of very old and younger canes. Climbing canes are generally a strange conglomeration of strong breaks and weak spurs (side growth). Many climbers possess zones of active growth that have migrated to stratospheric heights.

It takes knowledge, experience, and finesse to comprehend the tangled architecture of a climbing rose plant. Beginners should gain experience from pruning bush types, before they tackle climbers.

TWO DIFFERENT TYPE OF CANES; TWO DIFFERENT TYPES OF CLIMBERS

The climber designation includes two very different types of roses: pillar-type climbers and what I call the "traditional climbers." Each of these two types of climbing roses possesses physiological differences mark one as being significantly different from the other.

Those who seek to prune climbing roses well must learn how to distinguish the differences between the pillar-type climbers and the traditional climbers. This knowledge will help you to prune very large rose plants of all types.

PRIMOCANES AND FLORICANES

Members of the genus *Rosa* produce two main types of canes: primocanes and floricanes. Primocane roses bloom during their first year of growth. Floricane roses bloom during their second and subsequent years of growth.

I write about floricane roses in the "Pruning traditional climbers" section of this chapter. I write about primocane roses in the "Pruning pillar-type climbers" section of this chapter. Please read those chapters for information on those types of climbers.

PRUNING PILLAR-TYPE CLIMBERS

Most types of modern bush roses produce new canes that bloom during their first year of growth. This defines them as being primocane roses. This type of rose is easy to spot; their new canes terminate in a candelabra of blooms.

Some primocane roses are too tall to be classified as bushes. They are sometimes classified as shrubs or pillar-type climbers.

Confusing monikers aside, pillar-type climbers are wonderful garden plants. Climbers that bloom on their new canes get a gold-star rating from me. Instant gratification is a wonderful thing.

Anyone who grows or prunes pillar-type climbers *must* understand a basic concept: they are very tall bushes, not long, gangling climbers. Most pillar-type climbers aren't as vigorous as other varieties that are classified as climbers.

Pillar-type climbers should be pruned according to their growth habit and garden location. If they produce lots of new canes, remove about 25 percent of the older ones each year. If a plant doesn't produce new canes, don't remove any old ones.

Most pillar-type climbers produce flowering spurs (side shoots) on the nodes of their canes during their second and subsequent years of growth. Spurs are hard-working botanical machines.

Every hard-working machine that I ever used required maintenance. Rose spurs are no different. Some nodes produce several spurs. That can cause crowding. Each node should have just one spur. Remove the weakest and/or oldest spurs, and leave the strongest spur. Tip (cut back) the remaining spurs so that they have about four growth buds.

Every shoot on a rose plant *must* be pruned or tipped at pruning time. Small, large, short, long; every growing cane or stem must be headed back (cut) to a greater or lesser degree. This will force the plant's growth hormones into its side buds. That can result in growth of a desirable nature.

Be on the lookout for exhausted-node syndrome. For more information on that condition, see the "Exhausted-Node Syndrome" chapter in this book.

Don't use harsh pruning methods to induce pillar-type climbers into becoming larger plants. That might have a dwarfing effect on the plants.

Pruning traditional climbing roses

Most of the rose varieties that have been classified as climbers do *not* produce blooms on their new canes. This defines them as being floricane roses. I call roses of this type "traditional climbers."

Traditional climbers vary tremendously in terms of how they grow and bloom. That variance is the result of the climber designation's use as a lumper class.

The climbing sports of microminiatures, such as Climbing Si, produce new basal breaks that are only about three feet long. They grow and bloom just like traditional climbers, but on a smaller scale.

The *Rosa wichuraiana* hybrids are on the other end of the size scale. They can easily produce new basal breaks that grow forty feet or more in a single season. In subsequent years, new canes sometimes break from the ends of the old ones. In this fashion, *Rosa wichuraiana* roses can build themselves into barn-sized plants.

Some climbing varieties never stop expanding. Others reach a given height and then stop.

It would take a world of writing for me to put the theory of pruning traditional climbing roses into words. I don't have the time to write something of that nature. You probably don't have the time to read such a thing. I will do my best to explain it to you as concisely as I am able.

Climbers of all types should be pruned according to their growth habit and garden location. If the plants produce lots of new canes, remove about 25 percent of the older ones each year. If a given plant doesn't produce new canes, don't remove any old ones.

Large, overgrown or very old climbers are special beings. They should only be pruned by experienced hands. A few errant strokes with saw or shears can damage a special plant. The "Tread Softly with the Old" and "Pruning Very Large Plants" chapters of this book detail methodologies for pruning large, old, or overgrown plants.

Traditional climbers produce flowering spurs on the nodes of their canes during their second and subsequent years of growth. Rose spurs are hard-working botanical machines. They produce 100 percent of the flowers and most of the leaves on mature, traditional climbing rose plants.

Every hard-working machine that I ever viewed required maintenance. Rose spurs are no different. Some nodes will produce several spurs. That can cause crowding. Each node should have just one spur. Remove the weakest or oldest spurs, and leave the strongest spur. Tip (cut back) the remaining spurs so that they have about four growth buds.

Every shoot on a rose plant *must* be pruned or tipped at pruning time. Small, large, short, long; every growing cane or stem must be headed back (cut) to a greater or lesser degree. This will force the plant's growth hormones into its side buds. That can result in growth of a desirable nature.

Be on the lookout for exhausted-node syndrome. For more information on that condition, see the "Exhausted-Node Syndrome" chapter in this book.

MATCH CLIMBERS TO YOUR STATURE

I founded the garden that once housed the second-largest public collection of roses in the world. I was the top rosarian at another major public rose garden. I have advised and volunteered at a third major public rose garden.

Those gardens all shared a commonality: most of the people who were accomplishing day-to-day maintenance activities were women.

I quickly learned the benefit of growing the plants in *all* gardens, both public and private, at what I call "woman height." This makes it easier for women to maintain the plants. That, in turn means that the plants get more care. Easy pie, right?

Not quite. We all swoon when we see photos of twelve-foot-tall rose plants that are in full bloom. That kind of "plant porn" makes ambitious sorts want to do the same thing in our own gardens.

While monstrous roses might look good for a while, a price will eventually be exacted from their keepers. That price will be exacted when the monster plants need to be deadheaded or pruned.

Some gardeners believe they want a wild-land effect. "Just let the roses do as they will" is the motto of such people. That's a fun concept, *if* you have a five-acre garden (and grow the right varieties).

But most of us *don't* have five-acre gardens. That limiting factor alone means that we might be inclined to keep our rose plants at manageable heights.

In my opinion, a plant's height is appropriate if it's keepers can easily reach its top parts without using a ladder. Yes, I realize that ladder less gardening is not possible in all situations. But I still believe it is best for garden caretakers if most of the plants can be maintained while standing on the ground.

Pruning Shrub Roses

● ● ●

We are all but Chimpanzees-
That's a fact.
(Tho' you might dispute.)
Call us by another name,
We're all wearing monkey suits!

A SHRUB BY ANY NAME

ALL ROSE PLANTS ARE SHRUBS. Climbers are just overly ambitious shrubs.

Why don't we just classify every rose on Earth as a shrub? Because there are too many different families and types of roses to put into one big bag. That's why we have a hybrid this and a hybrid that. It makes things easier to follow.

Modern roses are a complex amalgam of different species. The children of these complex hybrids don't always fit into any classification. Taxonomists indicate that mixed-up varieties need to be classified as *something*. They *must* be plugged into a pigeonhole.

Rose varieties of an indefinite type are sometimes lumped into the shrub category. Yes, folks, there's that ol' lumper class thing, again. If you can't define a variety's type, lump it in with the shrubs. Confusing nomenclature aside, there is nothing wrong with this concept. There are some great shrub roses.

Growers need to know what kind of shrubs are in their gardens. This can help them to provide specific care to each variety.

"Knowing what you're growing" helps at pruning time. Read the "Pruning the Two Main Types of Climbers" chapter in this book. Many shrubs have more in common with climbers than with their bush counterparts.

Pruning Old Garden Roses and Other Exotic Types

●　　●　　●

Magic land,
Axle's center,
It's what they call that place.

At last removed
From Europe's darkness.
Still wandering in its shade.
China.

JUST HOW CHINESE ARE YOUR ROSES?

IN THE LATE EIGHTEENTH CENTURY, the genus *Rosa* received an infusion of genes that changed its members, forever. New roses arrived in Europe from China, which bloomed repeatedly and had marvelous, high-centered blooms.

The Chinese roses were used to breed many all-new classes of roses. Some of those new classes were created specifically to imbue the tender, subtropical Chinese roses with a measure of cold hardiness. In that regard, rose breeders have succeeded: repeat-blooming roses now thrive in areas that have very cold winters.

Every rose variety and type possesses its own set of unique traits. Some of those traits can be directly attributed to the proportion of Chinese rose genes that a given variety contains. Many varieties that contain a high percentage of pure Chinese rose genes are not exceptionally cold hardy.

The Bourbon, China, tea, and Noisette classes, all have members that have a high percentage of pure Chinese genes. Most of the members of those classes are not very cold hardy. Some of them resent hard pruning.

PRUNING BUSH FORMS OF CHINAS AND TEAS
Some Chinas and teas grow like weeds. Others are weaklings that require time to become established in the garden.

Many Chinas and teas have soft canes; such types generally resent hard pruning. This combination of traits makes Chinas and teas tricky to prune and unforgiving of mistakes.

Do *not* prune Chinas and teas as heavily as you might their close relatives, the hybrid teas, floribundas, and grandifloras.

Don't prune Chinas and teas much in any one year. Proceed slowly and knowledgeably. In this fashion, you can give your plants the time they need to grow and heal. This will also give you the chance to learn at a comfortable pace.

Many Chinas and teas don't produce a lot of new basal breaks. Do *not* casually remove canes from those types of roses; they might not ever be replaced. A diminished plant is the frequent result, when Chinas and teas receive hard pruning. It gets worse from there; Chinas and teas are prone to serious cane dieback, when they are pruned below the dogleg.

Susan Louise is a modern tea. That variety is my poster child for varieties that suffer cane dieback from pruning. I almost always get serious dieback when I cut the canes of Susan Louise. My response to that problem is simple; I seldom trim her canes.

Never cut below the dogleg on any type of rose. That rule is *especially* important with the Chinas and teas. Leave long stubs, paint your cuts, and hope for the best.

PRUNING DAMASKS AND PORTLANDS
The damasks and Portlands are closely related classes. They are sometimes lumped together for historical and horticultural purposes.

There is a tremendous amount of variation within these two classes. Some have short, stiff canes. Others are vigorous climbers. Some members of these classes bloom continuously. Others have just one bloom cycle, each year.

I recommend that you adjust pruning methods to the ways in which individual damasks and Portlands grow. Very dwarf types, such as Comte de Chambord, should be pruned in much the same fashion as low-growing hybrid teas.

If a plant is not growing vigorously, don't remove any canes. Tip every stem, cane, and sprout. Pull off the leaves, and call it a day.

Intermediate, repeat-blooming, bushy types of damasks and Portlands should also be pruned like hybrid teas. If intermediate types grow long canes, head them back. The canes will produce more blooms.

Many damasks and Portlands produce very long canes. Some of that type put their energy into growth, not bloom. When Joasine Hanet (also known as The Portland from Glendora) grows unchecked, she doesn't repeat bloom in a reliable fashion. Keep Joasine Hanet and varieties of like kind pruned back to four-foot shrubs. They should thank you with plenty of bloom.

Some Portlands do not produce an abundance of new basal breaks. They still need to be pruned with plant renewal in mind. Once again, time and experience will teach you what each variety requires to thrive.

PRUNING ALBAS, CENTIFOLIAS, AND GALLICAS

When it comes to pruning albas, centifolias, and gallicas, there are two different schools of thought. The old way indicates that they should be pruned in late spring, after their single blooming cycle is complete.

Many gardeners now prune albas, centifolias, and gallicas with their other roses (fall, winter, or early spring, as is appropriate in your area). I believe that this method is better.

It is generally easy to prune well-grown albas, centifolias, and gallicas. Remove most of the old canes (if young replacements are available). Tip the remaining canes, pull off any remaining leaves, and you're done.

In many climates, albas, centifolias, and gallicas should *not* be grown by the faint of heart! These classes can be *very* invasive. These roses can quickly overgrow their neighbors in the garden.

If the plants are growing out further from their centers than is desired, ruthlessly dig out, and remove the inevitable suckers.

Caution! Be extremely careful if you grow albas, centifolias, and gallicas as part of a collection. Do not plant them close to other varieties that have similar-looking plants! If two or more adjacent varieties grow together, variety integrity will be lost!

Pruning Tree Roses

● ● ●

Magical lollypops,
False confections.
Sweet things made of dreams.

Pay the price,
For artifice created.
Will it be worth the cost?

DR. FRANKENSTEIN, THE ROSE GROWER

IN MY OPINION, TREE ROSES are the problem children of the rose world. That is because they are artificial botanical constructs. Wild tree roses are rare things.

Few rose varieties are truly suited to growing as tree roses, yet millions of tree roses have been sold, which were topped by inappropriate rose varieties. Why? Because inappropriate varieties sometimes have name recognition. Name recognition sells plants. Varietal suitability be damned. That is why we have been subjected to tree roses which are grafted to Mister Lincoln, Oklahoma, and Queen Elizabeth. I have seen gardeners react with horror as their new tree roses produced eight-foot canes on top of the three-foot canestock (trunk).

Then there's the opposite side of the tree rose spectrum; many rose varieties are dwarfed when they are grown as tree roses. Yes, the bud union is still two or three feet above the ground. But the growing portions of the plants are generally not as vigorous as they would be if they were sprouting from ground level. This dwarfing effect is sometimes appreciated. Most gardeners don't want to see six-foot canes emerging from the top of a three-foot tree rose. The dwarfing effect is quite pronounced when some rose varieties are grown as tree roses. It can result in a lack of new basal breaks.

This is yet another case wherein time, knowledge, and experience will help a grower. If you like tree roses, forge on. You will eventually get it right.

Tree roses are tough to prune correctly. The list of variables and potential pitfalls is almost infinite. I believe that anyone who wants to prune a tree rose should ask themselves the following questions:

Are you an accomplished pruner?

Have ever pruned a tree rose?

Is the target tree rose old or young?

How old are the canes?

How many of the canes are new?

Has the zone of active growth migrated to a higher level? How high?

Has the plant attained an undesirable height?

Is it a safety hazard?

The answers to the preceding questions will provide you with some much-needed baseline data. Proceed slowly from there. It will help you to decide how a given tree rose should be pruned.

GENERAL GUIDELINES FOR PRUNING TREE ROSES

Most tree roses don't produce large quantities of new canes. This means that growers must deal with a given plant's existing canes. Remove old canes *only* if new replacement canes of appropriate nature are present.

Established tree roses usually have elevated zones of active growth. That is a normal consequence for plants that don't produce many new canes. Plants need to grow somewhere. If they can't produce new growth down below, they will break from higher points on their canes.

Prune away higher breaks in favor of those that have sprouting from a lower point. This should help to maintain or lower the zone of active growth.

Most people prefer to grow their tree roses in a lollypop shape. Head back canes that extend beyond the outside perimeters of the desired profile. Do *not* allow tree roses to grow too tall. Overgrown tree roses look awkward when they grow out of proportion to their canestock height. Tall tree roses are quite susceptible to wind blow over. A smaller plant will present a smaller wind picture.

Make sure that the stakes and ties that support tree-rose canestocks are strong and secure. See the "Tying Standard Roses" chapter of this book for tips on staking and tying tree roses.

Rose plants require adequate quantities of water and fertilizer. This is especially true after they are pruned. Tree roses are no different. Treat them gently during the growing season, which follows any pruning operation.

Pruning Very Large Rose Plants

● ● ●

Old horse standing
In a field,
Mighty in his stance.

Gone from the traces,
(Pulling loads),
But still a thing to see.

A WORLD OF GIANTS

I COUNT MYSELF AS BEING blessed. I was raised under and around enormous plants from the greater Rose family. Some of those giants were garden roses gone berserk. When I was young, I regularly observed a plant of Mermaid that overtopped a seventy-foot-tall palm tree. I was stunned to see large, yellow blooms far above my head.

That memory drove me to create my own giant plants. I covered the front sides of a two-story apartment building with plants of Mermaid and *Rosa chinensis* "Mutabilis." The plants were forty-five feet wide and twenty-five feet tall. Their main canes were thicker around than a man's waist. Those building-covering espaliers were a neighborhood landmark for almost forty years.

I love to prune very large rose plants. It is something akin to a religious experience for me. That is a good mind-set for someone who prunes oversized rose plants. Large rose plants should be treated as rare and precious things.

Most rose plants that are grown in garden situations eventually require pruning of one sort or another. Plants that grow to very large sizes are seldom granted an exemption to this rule.

I believe that anyone who wants to prune a very large rose plant should ask themselves the following questions:

Why are you pruning a given plant?

Has the plant become a safety hazard? (Safety trumps all other considerations, in the garden.)

Is the need for pruning of a chronic nature, such as annual maintenance?

Is the need for pruning of an acute nature?

Did a man-made or natural-support structure collapse?

Are you an accomplished pruner?

Have you ever pruned a very large rose plant?

The answers to the preceding questions will provide you with some much-needed baseline data. They will help you to decide whether you should prune a given rose plant.

PROCEED SLOWLY, *IF* YOU CAN

My main motto with large or old plants is "Tread softly with the old." (Please read the chapter that bears that name in this book.) In my estimation, "tread softly" means "prune slowly." I prefer to use a five-year pruning cycle with old, large, or overgrown rose plants.

Sadly, we don't always get that much time. When thorny canes block garden access points, quick action is sometimes required. Garden mechanics and safety trumps plant health considerations.

My general rules with pruning very large plants are quite basic:

Cut above a vigorous lower cane, if you can.

Leave long stubs on large cuts. If you cut a rose cane that is two or more inches thick, leave a stub that is eight to twelve inches long. Long stubs lessen the possibility that dieback will occur behind the growth eye. See the "Long Stubs Are Ugly but Beneficial" chapter of this book.

Very large rose plants are sometimes produced from climbing varieties. Please read the "Pruning the Two Main Types of Climbers" chapter of this book.

Rose plants require adequate quantities of water and fertilizer. This is especially true after they are pruned. Very large rose plants are no different. Treat them gently during the growing season, which follows any pruning operation.

Deadheading and Other Types of Summer Pruning

● ● ●

Seasons mark
The passing years.
Each one here-
Then gone.

IT'S ABOUT TIME

EVERY TEMPERATE CLIMATE IS MEASURED in terms of its number of frost-free days. Roses begin to grow in earnest when frosty nights go away. A clock begins ticking when the growing season begins. It is counting off the hours before the growing season ends.

If you deadhead a typical hybrid tea in July, it will generally produce another flush of blooms in mid-August. That's another kind of garden clock.

If you *don't* deadhead some roses, they will *not* repeat bloom. That is lost bloom and lost time. Neither you nor your plants will never regain that little bit of lost bloom time. The bloom clock stopped—but the seasonal clock did *not*.

EYES IN THE GARDEN

Deadheading is all about opportunity. When you are in your garden, you notice what is going on with your plants. When you are with your plants, you can make small changes that sometimes enable big results. A cut here can remove a weak stem. A cut there will give priority to a strong, new break.

EARLY-SEASON DEADHEADING

Ah, the first flush of bloom in the Spring! Was there ever a thing so sublime? Sadly, all things fade, including our roses. Please don't wax poetic about the faded blooms on your plants; cut them quickly so more blooms can follow.

Note how your plants are growing. Make minor adjustments in the water and fertilizer cycle, as needed.

SUMMER PRUNING

Winter pruning is about cleaning, refurbishing, and making way for new canes. Summer pruning is about minor corrections and setting up for the last bloom cycle of Autumn.

Go a little more slowly when you deadhead your roses in late summer. Take the time to note how the plants are growing. You will probably note some twiggy growth, here and there. Cut below such growth to a stronger stem. The plants will usually respond with superior bloom.

DON'T PRUNE HARD!

Summer is *not* the season for hard pruning. Go easy on your plants. They need their stems and leaves to make the plants stronger. Autumn is just around the corner.

Tying Roses Is Serious Business

● ● ●

Fiber's hold
Upon our clothing
Warp and weft, sublime.

All made from thread,
From varied sources,
Each different in its way.

Help me

ROSE PLANTS AREN'T ALWAYS CAPABLE of supporting their various parts. They sometimes need "a little support from a friend." (My apologies to the Beatles.) The parts that require support can sometimes be quite trivial; a drooping bloom can be made lovely with a piece of twine and a skilled knot. Sometimes the parts are critical; tree roses rest upon a single trunk. Twine and knots are the only lifeline to the all-important central stake. Lose the twine/lose the knot/lose the tree.

Plant tying is not a complicated operation. There is little to know. It comes down to three simple concepts: use the right tying material; use the right knot; know when to replace knots and stakes.

USE THE RIGHT TYING MATERIAL

String, twine, rope, and tape of all descriptions are used to tie plants. I lump those commodities into a single category, tying material.

Material selection is *the* most important aspect of tying plants. You can sometimes tie a bad knot with good material and still have a satisfactory outcome. If you tie a good knot with bad material, you probably will *not* enjoy a good outcome.

Roses grow outdoors. The materials that are used to tie them are exposed to the ravages of weather and sunlight. Weather means moisture. Moisture rots organic fibers. Don't use natural tying materials such as cotton, sisal, hemp, or Manila hemp. They won't last, out in the elements.

Synthetic tying materials are the way to go, in my opinion. They don't rot when they are exposed to moisture. That part of our tying material consideration is easy to solve.

The effects of sunlight on tying material is a tougher problem to overcome. Sunlight contains ultraviolet (UV) radiation. Many types of synthetic materials degrade when they are exposed to UV. Use tying materials that are resistant to UV radiation.

I use three different tying materials for my plants: tape, twine, and rope.

Around 99 percent of the plant tying in my gardens and nursery is accomplished with half-inch by eight mil vinyl tying tape. It is easy to use. The soft texture of vinyl tape is easy on tender, young stems.

Vinyl tape isn't well suited to supporting dead weight. Do *not use* vinyl tape to support large, heavy canes.

I use UV-rated twine for large plant parts. I know a tie that is made with 1/8-inch black agricultural twine will hold a heavy, old cane.

I use UV-rated quarter-inch rope to tie very heavy or special plants, such as standard (tree) roses. The thick cross section of rope provides gentle contact with large, heavy canes.

TYING MACHINES

Tying machines (tapeners) are marvelous things. Tapeners enable skilled users to make at least ten ties in the time it would normally take to make just one.

Tapeners are also quite tricky to use and difficult to maintain. In my opinion violins and tapeners have much in common; they are effective implements if you practice, but horrible to behold, if you don't.

A DANGEROUS MISCONCEPTION

Many folks believe is a safe material to use for tying rose plants. Guess what? Plants can be strangled by just about *any* tying material—*if* the tie is left intact for an extended time. Yes, I include soft, vinyl tape on the list of items potentially dangerous to plants.

Every tie on every plant must be renewed, each year. Be on the lookout for older ties that might have been missed or forgotten. Forgotten ties are silent plant killers!

USE THE RIGHT KNOT

Knot tying is a very detailed craft. The work is as much about the hands as it is the mind. I can't teach you very much about knot tying via the written word. Would-be plant tiers should find someone to teach them how to tie knots. That's the best way, in my estimation.

If you don't want to learn knot tying, you can still tie plants. How? Use an old-fashioned overhand or granny knot. Properly tied granny knots should be as durable as the material on which they are tied.

HOW TIGHT OF A KNOT?

Ties are used to support plant parts. If the tie is too loose, the support is lost. If the tie is too tight, the cane is lost.

Vinyl tape stretches. It can be pulled snugly around a stem. When the stem grows, the tape will stretch *a little* (But tape won't stretch much, before it begins to cut into stems, beware!)

Twine and rope usually don't stretch. If a plant part expands, twine and rope *won't*. Tight ties that are made with any material will cut off the circulation of vital, life-giving fluids. Injury or death can occur, when that happens.

I use what I call a "double wrap tie" with one-eighth-inch twine or quarter-inch rope. This means that I go around the cane and support mechanism twice, before tying the knot. This allows the plant's growing cane room to grow.

WHEN SHOULD TIES BE REPLACED?

This one is easy; replace every tie on every plant every year. There are *no* exceptions to this rule.

GENERAL METHODS FOR TYING ROSE PLANTS

I could write a book on tying rose plants. The topic is huge. But I don't have the time to write that kind of a book—and you don't have the time to read suchlike.

I have included information about tying and training roses in different chapters in this book. Those chapters include "Tying Tree Roses," "Growing, Training, and Tying Climbing Roses," and "Growing, Training, and Pruning Roses on Arbors and Pergolas."

I recommend you read those chapters, even if you don't intend to grow those types of roses. The tips that those chapters contain will help you to be a better gardener. Meanwhile, I'm going to provide you with a few, simple tips about tying roses.

QUICK TYING TIPS

Use several smaller ties on long or heavy canes. Don't depend on just one or two ties.

Don't pull canes too hard; they might crack. Try to make do with the natural position of a given cane, if you can.

Use temporary stakes to support heavy blooms or weak, new canes.

Tie new basal breaks as soon as is safely possible. New bend or break quite easily.

Use vertical or horizontal galvanized steel wires as quick, simple trellises.

Tying Tree Roses

● ● ●

No man stands alone-
(We all can use some help.)
Remember that which keeps us upright
So we will not fall.

TREE ROSES ARE *VERY* COMPLEX organisms. Growers produce plants that have one, long cane. They then graft a desirable variety high up on the cane. The original cane becomes a canestock (trunk). Few people give much thought about the trunks of their tree roses. They are forgotten.

But there's a problem with that mind-set. People grow roses on canestock to create trees. Roses didn't evolve to become trees. Roses evolved to be shrubs and gangly climbers.

When natural rose plants grow large, they generally require support. Tree roses are no different. The root systems and canestocks of tree roses do not possess the strength to safely hold the plants upright.

Stakes must be used to support tree roses. But here's another problem: stakes are supporting a largely forgotten portion of a rose tree's anatomy. Stakes are even more forgettable. Many gardeners stake tree roses and assume all will go well from there.

But that's not the way that it works. Most people use wooden stakes with their tree roses. *All* types of wooden stakes will rot. The visible, aboveground portion of a given stake might appear to be sound. But the invisible (weight-supporting) portion, which lies under the ground, might be rotten. This can lead to hidden danger for the plants that depend on rotten stakes for their survival. Do *not* use wooden stakes to tie the canestocks (trunks) of tree roses!

I use extruded steel T fence posts or number-eight (0.79 inch) steel-reinforcing rods to stake tree roses. Both of those materials are inexpensive to buy and easy to use. They are quite durable when they are used as plant stakes.

I have found that extruded steel T posts are more durable than number-eight rebar. T posts have stabilizing wings at the bottom. These will cut the root systems of established plants. I use extruded steel fence posts *only* with newly planted tree roses.

I use a number-eight reinforcing rod to stake established tree roses. It's smaller, cylindrical shape does less damage to established root systems.

A FOOLPROOF METHOD FOR STAKING NEWLY PLANTED TREE ROSES

Dig a planting hole for the tree rose. Drive a temporary marker stake in the exact desired position of the plant. Place a five-foot-long extruded steel T post about two inches behind the marker stake. Drive the post into its final position. The top of the steel post should be about 1.5 to 2 inches below the desired level of the tree rose's top bud union (where the growing portion of the plant meets the canestock).

Caution! Extruded steel T posts absorb solar radiation. The posts can become quite hot. Damage to the canestock will occur if it contacts hot metal! Steel stakes must not be allowed to touch a tree rose's canestock!

PVC pipe makes an excellent insulator. It will protect canestocks from hot metal stakes. I use 1¼ inch, schedule 40 PVC as an insulator on most extruded steel T posts.

Caution! There are many different types of steel fence posts. Stamped steel fence posts corrode quite rapidly. Do not use stamped steel fence posts to stake tree roses. Use only extruded steel fence posts to stake tree roses.

A FOOLPROOF METHOD FOR STAKING ESTABLISHED TREE ROSES

Drive a piece of number-eight steel-reinforcing rod (rebar) about two inches away from the tree roses' canestock. The top of the reinforcing rod should be about 2.5 inches below the level of the top-bud union (where the growing portion of the plant meets the canestock).

Caution! Extruded steel T posts absorb solar radiation. The posts can become quite hot. Damage to the canestock will occur if it contacts hot metal! Steel stakes must not be allowed to touch a tree rose's canestock!

PVC pipe makes an excellent insulator. It will protect canestocks from hot metal stakes. I use one-inch, schedule 40 PVC as an insulator on number-eight reinforcing-rod stakes.

Slip the PVC pipe over the reinforcing rod (after the rod has been driven into the planting hole). The top of the PVC pipe should be about 2.5 inches lower than the top of the reinforcing rod. This will leave three inches of the T post exposed. The portion of the reinforcing rod that rises above the PVC shield is critical. It will provide you an excellent attachment point for the ties that bind the tree rose to the stake.

PAINT THE HEAT SHIELD

PVC pipe degrades when it is exposed to direct sunlight. Paint the heat shield with two coats of a high-quality, water-based primer. After the PVC insulator has been primed, you can use a finish coat in any color that you prefer. I paint the heat shield before I slip it over the steel stake.

TYING TREE ROSES TO SHIELDED STEEL STAKES

"The top tie is the main guy." I coined that little ditty as a memory aid. It reminds me that the top tie on a standard rose plant is critical.

The bottom ties help to reduce canestock flex. But they won't do much to prevent blow over/blowout damage to standard roses.

I use UV-rated, quarter-inch black poly rope for the top ties on my tree roses. It presents a wide surface to the canestock. This means it will not cut into the bark of the plant.

I use figure-eight ties; one loop of the number eight is around the canestock. The other loop is around the stake. I then wrap the ends of the rope totally around the canestock/stake combination (twice). I then tie a good, stout knot. The knot must be tight enough to securely hold the canestock, but not tight enough to cut into the bark.

I recommend using a second figure-eight tie down lower on the canestock.

Caution! There is no safe tying material! Renew all plant ties every year. Be on the lookout for old ties that you previously missed. Old, forgotten ties are silent plant killers!

Caution! Don't make ties too tight! They will constrict the canestock and cut off the flow of nutrient fluids!

Caution! Don't make ties too loose! They will slip and fail to hold the canestock!

Growing, Training, and Tying Climbing Rose Plants

●　●　●

Conjure up a woodland sight,
In an urban space.
Your eyes made whole
By greensward color-
That a saving grace.

Infinity

THERE ARE AN INFINITE NUMBER of methods by which climbing roses can
be grown, trained, and tied. An infinite number of materials exist that can
be used to support and tie rose plants. There is a finite quantity of space
available in this book for me to use to teach you about rose plant tying and
training techniques. Read on; I will do my best to provide you with a few
insights.

HOW A CLIMBER WILL BE GROWN DETERMINES HOW IT WILL BE TRAINED AND TIED

Climbing roses can be grown in many ways. Each of them has its own
growing, training, and tying method. Those methods vary greatly in
the amount of planning and training that they require. Some methods for growing climbers are basic and easy. Others are detailed and
complex.

The sprawl method of growing climbing rose plants

I was raised in rose-family paradise. I have seen countless rose plants that spread and sprawled over fences, trees, and outbuildings. In Central California, Belle of Portugal, Climbing Cecile Brunner, Mermaid, and various *Rosa banksia* cultivars are commonly grown in this way.

The plants vary in size from twelve to two hundred feet. In the fields, feral roses assume massive ball-like forms. They are lovely in the spring. I know of an old French rambler that climbs and trails over several acres of creek-side treetops. Its blooms wink down from fifty feet. What an incredible sight.

Most of the untrained, gigantic rose plants I have observed received no human-directed irrigation. They bloom in the spring, with the rains, and then wait for another year.

Some of the gigantic rose plants I have seen are forgotten relics from someone's long-gone garden. Others are carefully orchestrated creations.

I have developed a methodology for growing roses au natural; I call it "the sprawl method of growing climbing roses." This is the easiest method for growing climbing roses. Little or no training or tying is involved. The roses grow where they will.

The sprawl method requires the right rose variety and a lot of garden space. If you grow plants in an area that does not receive rain during the growing season, you will also need a good irrigation system.

Sprawling roses fall into two categories: those that receive regular pruning and those that do not.

Sprawling roses that will receive no pruning are growing in a natural state. Such plants are said to be *naturalized*. Naturalized roses are left to their own devices. They are encouraged to grow (and grow, grow, grow). If the plants reach into places where they are unwanted or unsafe, someone prunes them back.

I believe that *all* rose plants benefit from educated, knowledgeable pruning. That's why I prefer to prune sprawling roses each winter. It rejuvenates the plants and provides more bloom. It also reduces the possibility that the plants will be infected with fungal diseases. Follow the guidelines in the "Pruning the Two Main Types of Climbers" chapter of this book.

Sprawling roses are untrained, but they are still roses. This means that they require adequate quantities of water and fertilizer. Untrained roses sometimes form thickets. How to you get into a thicket to water the mother plant? Install a drip system.

How do you weed a thicket if the plants are trying to kill you? Don't weed the plants; install a thick mulch, instead. Four to six inches of wood chips will prevent most weed seeds from germinating.

The Count Dracula method of growing climbers

Climbing roses have never enjoyed the popularity of their bush counter-parts. Most people believe that their gardens are just too small to include climbing rose plants. I counter that sentiment with the following knowl-edge: climbing rose plants don't have to be huge things. There are climb-ers that grow in a restrained fashion. More importantly, there are ways to grow climbers that allow them to be grown in small spaces.

My favorite of these is the Count Dracula method of growing climbing rose plants. Why have I come up with such a silly name for a plant-growing methodology? Because I drive a stake through the heart of the plants!

This allows me to grow climbing rose plants as pillars. The term "pil-lar" refers to a rose plant that is grown as a tall, narrow column. I have writ-ten about pillar-type climbers elsewhere in this book. Please do not confuse those two definitions. See "pillar" and "pillar-type climber" in the glossary.

Pillars are nearly forgotten relics. They are fading reminders of gar-dening traditions that date back hundreds of years. Pillars have tradition-ally been planted because of space considerations. People never seem to have enough growing area in their gardens. Every garden seems to contain flawed, little niches.

Old-time gardeners planted climbers in disused little spaces. They drove a six-foot stake behind the plants. This was used to hold the canes in a vertical position. When the canes overtopped the stake, they were headed back. The result was a six-foot mass of foliage and blooms.

An easy way to grow rose pillars

Growing pillars requires a good deal of thought, but very little labor. Select a climbing rose variety that is known to have a modest growth habit. Make sure that the variety is one that thrives in your area. See the "Which rose varieties are suitable for growing as pillars?" section of this chapter.

Dig a planting hole. Drive a temporary marker stake in the exact, desired position of the climber. Place an eight-foot-long, extruded steel T post about three inches behind the marker stake. Drive the post into its final position. The top of the steel post should be about six feet above the ground. (Two feet of the post will lie below the surface of the soil.)

Caution! Extruded steel T steel posts absorb solar radiation. The posts can become quite hot. The canes will be damaged if they contact hot metal! Steel stakes must not be allowed to touch the growing parts of any plant!

PVC pipe makes an excellent insulator. It will prevent rose canes from being burned by hot metal stakes. I use 1¼ inch, schedule 40 PVC as an insulator on most extruded steel T posts.

Slip the PVC pipe over the T post (after the post has been driven into the planting hole). The top of the PVC pipe should be about 2.5 inches lower than the top of the T post. This will leave 2.5 inches of the T post exposed. The portion of the T post that rises above the PVC shield is critical. It will provide you an excellent attachment point for the ties that bind the canes to the stake.

Caution! There are many different types of steel fence posts. Stamped steel fence posts corrode quite rapidly. Do not use stamped steel fence posts to stake rose plants. Use only extruded steel fence posts to stake rose plants.

Paint the heat shield

PVC pipe degrades when it is exposed to direct sunlight. Paint the heat shield with two coats of a high-quality, water-based primer. After the PVC insulator has been primed, you can use a finish coat in any color that you prefer. I paint the heat shield before I slip it over the steel stake.

How to train pillar roses

Pillar roses are finite constructions. They must be confined into fixed, compact forms. Tie a pillar's canes so that they stand vertically. No, don't cram them together like the stems in a broom. Space them so that they radiate around the stake. Space the canes a few inches apart. The cross section of the canes and stake should be about twelve to eighteen inches in diameter.

Tie the canes when they are young. Rose canes have a memory. They also become harder as they grow. Don't use too much force when you bend the canes for tying. Young rose canes are easy to break.

A typical six-foot cane should be supported by at least three ties. See the "Tying Roses Is Serious Business" chapter of this book.

Which rose varieties are suitable for growing as pillars?

Pillars are used to create garden focal points. Pillars incorporate large rose varieties into small gardens. But there is a downside to all of this. Pillars exist in a *very* defined world. Most of them are required to fit into small spaces. Pillars are like supermodels; they *must* forever maintain a specified profile or look—or they are out of job.

It all comes down to variety selection. If you want to be a supermodel, it helps to be six feet tall, slim, and gorgeous. Pillar rose candidates need similar characteristics. They should thrive when they are grown as narrow, six- to eight-foot plants. The canes should be long and straight, not short and bushy. The canes of pillars must be of a type that tolerates being forced into a severe, vertical position.

Pillar candidates should have gorgeous foliage. It helps if they are of types that have foliage and blooms all the way to the ground.

Roses that are grown as pillars should be particularly disease resistant. Remember, their canes are not spread out. Pillar canes are pulled together, a few inches apart. There isn't much room for air circulation in such a construct.

I prefer to grow sterile or semi sterile varieties as pillars. That type of rose doesn't set very many hips. Such behavior for easier and safer plant maintenance. See the "Deadheading and Summer Pruning" chapter in this book for tips on deadheading large plants.

A FEW VARIETIES THAT MAKE EXCELLENT ROSE PILLARS

Pillars have been grown for all sorts of reasons. Sometimes folks just want to make a troublesome plant fit into the garden. Folks who carefully plan to create a lovely garden focal point are lucky. They can select a variety that is perfectly suited to growing as a pillar.

I have compiled a short list of varieties that make excellent rose pillars. This list is not complete. I encourage you all to go out and find varieties that make good rose pillars. Experiment a little. It might be fun.

Climbing Angel Face. Climbing Floribunda. Angel Face sport. Haight. 1981.
Antike 89. Climber. Kordes. 1989.
Barbara Worl (also known as Grandmother's Hat). Found rose. Date of introduction unknown.
Crepuscule. Noisette. Dubreuil. 1904.
Duchesse d'Auerstadt. Noisette. Reve d'Or sport. Bernaix. 1888.
Excellenz von Schubert. Polyantha. Lambert. 1909.
Elmshorn. Shrub. Kordes. 1951.
Fourth of July. Large-Flowered Climber. Carruth. 1999.
Gene Boerner. Floribunda. Boerner. 1968.
Golden Showers. Large-Flowered Climber. Lammerts. 1956.
Climbing Kaiserin Auguste Viktoria. Kaiserin Auguste Viktoria sport. Dickson. 1897.
Climbing Lady Hillingdon. Climbing Tea. Lady Hillingdon sport. Hicks. 1917.

Lamarque. Noisette. Marechal. 1830.

Lost Rainbows (Synonym; Larry Daniels). Barbara Worl sport. Liggett. 2016.

Climbing Maman Cochet. Climbing Tea. Date of introduction unknown.

Climbing Margo Koster. Margo Koster sport. Golie. 1962.

Oranges 'n Lemons. Shrub. Mc Gredy. 1985.

Climbing Old Blush. Climbing China. Old Blush sport. Circa 1752.

Climbing Pompon de Paris. Climbing Miniature. Pompon de Paris sport. Date of introduction unknown.

Red Fountain. Large-Flowered Climber. Williams. 1975.

Renae. Climbing Floribunda. Moore. 1954.

Rhonda. Large-Flowered Climber. Lissemore. 1968.

Rosa chinensis mutabilis. China. Date of introduction unknown. Possibly an ancient variety.

Rosarium Euetersen. Climber. Kordes. 1977.

Royal Gold. Large-Flowered Climber. Morey. 1957.

Climbing Snowbird. Climbing Hybrid Tea. Snowbird sport. Weeks. 1949.

Sombreuil. Large-Flowered Climber. Wyant. Introduced circa 1959.

Souvenir de Claudius Denoyel. Climbing Hybrid Tea. Chambard. 1920.

Climbing Souvenir de la Malmaison. Climbing Bourbon. Souvenir de la Malmaison sport. Bennett. 1893.

Susan Louise. Shrub. Possibly a Belle Portugaise sport. Adams; introduced by Stocking. 1929.

Climbing White Maman Cochet. Climbing Tea. White Maman Cochet sport.

William Allen Richardson. Noisette. Reve d'Or sport. Ducher. 1878.

PRUNING PILLAR ROSES

I do not wish to repeat information that I have written in other places in this book. I recommend you read the "Pruning the Two Main Types of Climbers" chapter of this book.

Rose pillars are severe and regimented botanical constructions. The plants must never be allowed to grow beyond certain top and side limits. Pillars require frequent attention with shears and tying materials. Neglected pillars can quickly become sprawling climbers.

Pillars are much more appealing when they are covered with foliage, all the way to the ground. That's not going to happen if the zone of active growth migrates to a higher level. The zone of active growth *must* be maintained at a very low level.

TRAINING ESPALIERED CLIMBERS

Most climbers are grown as espaliers. This means that they are attached to a frame. Espaliered plants are usually two dimensional. This means that they are flat on one or more sides.

Espaliers are an ancient form of plant training. They are used for many purposes. Espaliered plants are sometimes planted next to walls. This creates warmer, more forgiving growing conditions for the plants. Espaliers are also used where garden space is limited. A large rose plant can be used in a small garden if it is espaliered.

TRELLISES

The structures that are used to support espaliered plants are called "trellises." Mankind has used trellises for thousands of years. They have been built out of just about every natural and manufactured material on earth. I am not going to mention most of them in this book.

I use just two kinds of trellises, wooden and wire.

Wooden trellises vary widely in the construction and material makeup. Some are vast confections of redwood or cedar. Most trellises are made from cast-off lumber, sticks, or tree branches. I seldom use wooden trellises. They are far too impermanent for my uses.

Wire trellises are my plant-supporting mechanism of choice. I stretch wires from the eaves of buildings to anchors in the ground. I stretch wires between nails that are embedded in wooden fences. I stretch wires between extruded steel T posts. Those types of wire trellises all do the same thing; they provide long-lived attachment points for rose plants.

CANE ANGLE IS CRUCIAL

This concept is easy; rose canes don't do well when they are bent below a forty-five-degree angle. Canes that grow parallel to the ground are prone to sunburn. Sunburned canes might not die, but they *will* lose vigor. Canes should spread up in a fan shape. This allows plenty of room for air circulation and future plant growth.

USE SEVERAL TIES

Don't use just one or two ties to support long or heavy rose canes. Use several ties. This will spread the load between several attachment points. If one tie breaks, the cane will not normally break.

TIE CANES IMMEDIATELY

Rose plants naturally grow as bushy shrubs, *not* manicured, two-dimensional espaliers. Vigorous rose plants will try to outgrow the confines of a trellis. Tie new canes as soon as they are produced. Rose canes are generally more pliable when they are young.

KEEP PLANTS AT A MANAGEABLE HEIGHT

Rose plants thrive best when they receive regular trimming. It's tough to prune gigantic plants. It's also *dangerous* to trim gigantic plants. Ladders are dangerous tools, *especially* in the garden.

Grow your plants at heights that are easy for you to maintain. Your plants will thrive. Your local orthopedic surgeon might be denied a job or ten.

Growing Roses on Arches and Pergolas

● ● ●

Lost dream ruin,
On the land.
Broken humps of stone.
In the midst,
A temple's glory.
Reveals what we have lost.
Roman Forum.

SCENES FROM A BYGONE AGE

AH, BUT HERE'S A SUBJECT to fill a book. Sadly, I have just a few lines to share with you on the matter.

Arches and pergolas share a common function; they are structures that allow human traffic to pass below an overhang of living rose plants.

Arches and pergolas vary widely in their forms and how they are defined. My own definitions of these constructs are somewhat relaxed.

Most arches are small structures. They have just two sides and a rounded or square top. I call that type of structure an arch.

If an arch is much larger, I call it a pergola. Pergolas vary in size, structure, and shape. Some are six-feet wide by eight-feet tall. That is almost small enough to be called a "small arch."

Some pergolas are barn sized. Others are hundreds of feet long.

THE ULTIMATE FORM OF CLIMBING ROSE

The plants that grow on arches and pillars are the monarchs of climbing roses. They wrap every desirable rose trait into one, massive package. They tie it all together with confetti-like ribbons of falling rose petals.

Arches and pergolas are relics of a bygone age. People once had the time to build gardens and stroll under their roses. Those who plant or maintain arches and pergolas are fortunate; they know they have recaptured the charm of days gone by. I hope that some of you will indulge yourselves by building a garden structure.

VARIETY SELECTION IS EVERYTHING

The relative success or failure of rose arches and pergolas frequently comes down to one consideration, variety selection. Why is that true? Because rose arches and pergolas are finite botanical constructions. The plants that grow on such structures *must* meet certain criteria if they are going to thrive.

Criterion number one: The plant must cover the structure in a relatively short time. By my way of thinking, that's two or three years.

Criterion number two: The rose plant must *stop* growing when it has covered the structure. No, I don't mean that the plant should stop growing, altogether. (You don't want that.) But it must *not* be a type of rose that continuously tries to cover more and more space.

Criterion number three: The variety should be self-cleaning. This means spent blooms drop cleanly off the plant. You don't want ugly dead stuff hanging onto your lovely garden structure.

Criterion number four: Varieties that are used on arches and pergolas should also be sterile or semi sterile; they should set few (or no) hips. Trust the voice of experience, folks; deadheading arches and pillars is a nightmarish and dangerous job.

Criterion number five: Size is everything. People have their own selection criteria for roses. Some of them are basic. For example, someone might like a pink bush to go by their front door. That's an easy criterion to satisfy. There are thousands of pink bush roses.

Selecting varieties for use on arches and pergolas is a tougher thing. The requirements for such roses are rigid. Most of those requirements can be pared down to one concept, structure size. Just how big is a given arch or pergola? More importantly, how wide is the structure? Wide structures require rose varieties that can grow and build very long canes.

Rose varieties that are planted on wide structures must also have long-lived canes. Why? Because there is no way that people are going to prune out twelve- to twenty-foot long canes each year. This is a real "be true to yourself" moment.

No, I am not saying that large pergolas don't require annual winter pruning. It is my firm belief that every rose plant needs to be pruned, cut, or mowed each year.

Criterion number six: Cane age matters. Some varieties have canes that can live for many decades. Other varieties have canes that weaken after three or four years.

Plants that cover arches and pergolas fall into two categories: those that must have their canes replaced on a regular basis and those that do not.

I have a medium-sized pergola at my downtown San Jose main growing ground. It is planted with two of my proprietary clones of Sombreuil. The canes of Sombreuil do not age very well. They weaken and lose vigor in a relatively short time. I prune my plants of Sombreuil so that the canes are replaced about every five years. That's alright for my pergola. It is small enough to be covered with a variety like Sombreuil.

I would not use Sombreuil or a rose of like kind for a very large pergola. The canes would not live long enough to build onto each other and create a huge mass. I would choose a variety that has long-lived canes. The canes of such roses sometimes build onto each other. That would make it easier for the plant to cover a large pergola.

Most of the successful large rose structures I have seen were covered with happy, old canes.

Criterion number seven: Use an appropriate quantity of rose plants. This might seem to be a simple concept, but it apparently is *not*. Many of the arches I have seen were planted with a rose on just one side. The growers mistakenly believed that one vigorous plant would reach up, over, and down the structure.

Yes, I know, some varieties *are* vigorous enough to cover both sides of an arch. But roses didn't evolve to grow that way. Roses bloom better when they grow vertically or semi horizontally.

Criterion number eight: Mirror-image arches and pergolas *must* have identical varieties planted across from each other. The human eye innately follows texture and form. Every rose variety possesses its own, unique look. Mirror-image plantings appear to be out of balance when they are composed of different varieties.

Note: A mirror-image planting, which is comprised of a given variety and its sport, is sometimes acceptable. The two plants must have identical growth habits for this variant planting to be successful.

Criterion number nine: The variety should bloom repeatedly. This criterion was placed last in line for a reason; it is more flexible in its scope than the other criteria.

My gardens are all located in areas that have mild winters and long, benevolent summers. Because my gardens benefit from a long growing season, I love repeat-blooming roses.

But we must look out for the exceptions that life places at our feet. Exceptions sometimes add spice to the pot. Some once-blooming roses are excellent candidates for growing on arches and pergolas.

Most once-blooming roses bloom quite early in the season. An arch or pergola that is planted with such a rose will add a huge splash of early-season color to your garden.

I would *love* to see a large pergola that is covered with one of the *Rosa banksia* hybrids. It would be spectacular.

A *HORRIBLE* CHOICE FOR ARCHES AND PERGOLAS

I have seen hundreds of arches and pergolas. Most of them were planted with Climbing Cecile Brunner. I have seen hundreds of photographs that depict arches and pergolas. A high percentage of those photographs show that the structures are covered with Climbing Cecile Brunner.

You might be asking yourself, "What's the big deal, Tom? If everybody is planting Climbing Cecile Brunner, then it must be a great choice." "Everybody" is *wrong*, in this case.

The original, bush form of Cecile Brunner is one of *the* best rose varieties on earth. Several of its sports are excellent. But the climbing sport of Cecile Brunner is horrible. Why? For starters, Climbing Cecile Brunner never stops growing. It builds its thorny, long, thick canes onto each other with wild abandon.

Next, Climbing Cecile Brunner doesn't shed its spent blooms. They fade, dry, and hold on the plant for weeks or months. Last month's lovely spring bloom morphs into a brown, overlaying mass.

It gets worse from there; Climbing Cecile Brunner doesn't repeat bloom very well. Large, well established plants *will* scatter bloom throughout the season. But most clones of Climbing Cecile Brunner do *not* produce a decent flush of repeat bloom. That is not what you expect from a huge plant that is growing in a mild climate.

A PERGOLA OF NIGHTMARISH PROPORTIONS
Cautionary tales are good for the human psyche. They ground us in the reality of what can happen if we make certain choices.

Many years ago, a friend of mine obtained a grant to build a gymnasium-sized pergola in The San Jose Municipal Rose Garden. My friend announced she would cover that structure with Climbing Cecile Brunner.

I advised her of the various undesirable traits that the variety possesses. She chirped, "You are wrong, Tom. *Everybody* knows that Climbing Cecile Brunner is *the* best variety for growing on a pergola."

I pressed the issue. It turned into a big public discussion. My advice was roundly (and loudly) dismissed by everyone concerned. To a person, they all exclaimed, "You're wrong, Tom. *Everybody* knows that Climbing Cecile Brunner is *the* best variety for growing on a pergola."

I lost the argument. The pergola was planted with Climbing Cecile Brunner.

Fast-forward a few decades. The San Jose Municipal Rose Garden pergola has become a gigantic tunnel o' brambles. Climbing Cecile Brunner is seeking whole new vertical and horizontal realms to conquer. Workers regularly whack off errant canes that attempt to "decapitate" innocent passersby.

The San Jose Municipal Rose Garden pergola is scheduled to be replaced in late 2017. The plants of Climbing Cecile Brunner will be pruned and tied to the new pergola.

I'm all for replacing the pergola. But I believe it's a mistake to not remove the existing plants of Climbing Cecile Brunner. In my opinion, an opportunity is being squandered. A flawed, potentially dangerous variety could be replaced with one that that is safer and more appropriate.

Note to The City of San Jose: some great thornless or semi thornless vigorous rose varieties are out there. They are waiting for you to find them. I doubt that will happen. Why? The existing plants of Climbing Cecile Brunner are large and healthy.

Then there's the other consideration: *everybody* knows Climbing Cecile Brunner is the best variety for growing on a pergola.

A FEW GOOD VARIETIES FOR GROWING ON ARCHES AND PERGOLAS

I know of a few varieties that thrive when they are grown on arches and pillars. I'm certain that many more exist.

Follow the criteria that I have delineated elsewhere in this chapter. With a little work, you can find some other great varieties for growing on arches and pergolas.

VARIETIES FOR GROWING ON SMALL ARCHES AND PERGOLAS

Climbing Cramoisi Superieur. Climbing China. Cramoisi Superieur sport. Couturier. 1885.
Crepuscule. Noisette. Dubreuil. 1904.

Elmshorn. Shrub. Kordes. 1951.

Golden Showers. Large-Flowered Climber. Lammerts. 1956.

Climbing Maman Cochet. Climbing Tea. Date of introduction unknown.

Climbing Margo Koster. Climbing Polyantha. Margo Koster sport. Golie. 1962.

Climbing Rainbow's End. Climbing Miniature. Rainbow's End sport. O'Brien. 1998.

Climbing Lady Hillingdon. Climbing Tea. Lady Hillingdon sport. Hicks. 1917.

Lamarque. Noisette. Marechal. 1830.

Climbing Old Blush. Climbing China. Old Blush sport. Circa 1752.

Climbing Pompon de Paris. Climbing Miniature. Pompon de Paris sport. Date of introduction unknown.

Renae. Climbing Floribunda. Moore. 1954.

Rosarium Euetersen. Climber. Kordes. 1977.

Rosa chinensis mutabilis. China. Date of introduction unknown. Possibly an ancient variety.

Climbing Snowbird. Climbing Hybrid Tea. Snowbird sport. Weeks. 1949.

Sombreuil. Large-Flowered Climber. Introduced by Wyant, circa 1959.

Climbing Souvenir de la Malmaison. Climbing Bourbon. Souvenir de la Malmaison sport. Bennett. 1893.

Climbing White Maman Cochet. Climbing Tea. White Maman Cochet sport. Date of introduction unknown.

William Allen Richardson. Noisette. Reve d'Or sport. Ducher. 1878.

VARIETIES FOR GROWING ON LARGE ARCHES AND PERGOLAS
Aimee Vibert. Noisette. Vibert. 1828.

Belle Portugaise. Cayeux. 1903.

Bouquet d'Or. Noisette. Ducher. 1872.

Francois Juranville. Rambler. Barbier. 1906.

Lamarque. Noisette. Marechal. 1830.

Rosa chinensis mutabilis. China. Date of introduction unknown. Possibly an ancient variety.

Rosa banksiae banksiae. Species. Introduced in 1807. Possibly an ancient variety.

Rosa banksiae lutea. Species. Introduced in 1824. Possibly an ancient variety.

Rosa chinensis mutabilis. China. Date of introduction unknown. Possibly an ancient variety.

Elmshorn. Shrub. Kordes. 1951.

Lamarque. Noisette. Marechal. 1830.

TRAINING ROSE PLANTS TO GROW ON ARCHES AND PILLARS
CANE ANGLE IS CRUCIAL

This concept is easy; rose canes don't do well when they are bent below a forty-five-degree angle. Canes that grow parallel to the ground are prone to sunburn. Sunburned canes might not die, but they *will* lose vigor. Canes should spread up in a fan shape. This allows plenty of room for air circulation and future plant growth.

USE SEVERAL TIES

Don't use just one or two ties to support long or heavy rose canes. Use several ties. This will spread the load between several attachment points. If one tie breaks, the cane will not normally break.

TIE CANES IMMEDIATELY

Rose plants naturally grow as bushy shrubs, *not* manicured, two-dimensional espaliers. Vigorous rose plants will generally try to outgrow the confines of a trellis. Tie new canes and other types of desirable as soon as it is produced. Rose canes are generally more pliable when they are young.

PRUNING ROSE PLANTS THAT GROW ON ARCHES AND PILLARS

I do not want to repeat information that I have written in other places in this book. I recommend that you read the "Pruning the Two Main Types of Climbers" chapter of this book.

Rose arches and pergolas are rigidly defined botanical constructions. The plants must never be allowed to grow beyond certain top and side limits.

All rose plants grow best when they receive competent annual pruning. Roses that grow on arches and pillars are no different.

Arches and pillars require frequent attention with shears and tying materials. Neglected roses of any sort can quickly become sprawling climbers.

SAFETY TRUMPS ALL OTHER CONSIDERATIONS

Most of the people who read this chapter will do so in the comfort and safety of their own home. Everything looks easy from an easy chair. There is *no* aspect of pruning arches and pergolas that could be accurately described as being easy.

Compared to an adult human, the smallest rose arch is large. An average pergola is larger. Traditional, old-style pergolas are *huge*. How does one prune such things? How do you prune such things without breaking your neck? Very carefully—and with the right tools.

There was a time when all large rose-supporting structures were pruned by people who were standing on ladders. I know that is true. I had two mirror-image rose trellises at my old main garden. They were twenty-five feet tall and forty-five feet wide. I pruned those plants at least twenty times over a forty-year period. I accomplished the task while standing on ladders. I can emphatically state that I am lucky to have survived that set of experiences; it was *scary*.

Technology changed the world of pruning huge plants. Bucket lifts can put rose pruners right on top of a large structure. Bucket lifts are inexpensive to rent and easy to use.

Please read the "Garden Safety" chapter of this book before you proceed. It should help you grasp some important concepts.

THEY ARE HUGE, BUT THEY ARE STILL ROSES

People have a marked tendency to get lost when they stare at rose arches and pillars. The tangle of growth is like a gigantic bowl of Ramen noodles; how can you tell where one noodle starts and another one ends?

That kind of mind-lock is acceptable for a casual observer. But it won't work for the folks who must prune arches and pergolas.

And, yes arches and pergolas *must* be pruned, every year. That is because a rose that is grown in a spectacular way is still just a plant. Plants have very real physical needs—and limitations.

THE ZONE OF ACTIVE GROWTH AS REVISITED FROM A DIFFERENT PERSPECTIVE

There is a chapter in this book that is entitled "The Most Important Rose-Pruning Concept." It deals with what I have named the zone of active growth. I recommend you read that chapter before you proceed with this section.

Every rule seems to have at least one exception. My rule about maintaining a low zone of active growth is no different. Some arches and all pergolas will *benefit* from having an elevated zone of active growth. Why am I writing about this exception?

Because few rose varieties possess the vigor that is needed to produce new ground-level basal breaks that are long enough to go up and over a large structure. The canes must build onto one another, to cover space and distance. That kind of coverage is generally results from canes that are in the second and subsequent years of growth. That kind of cane usually has an elevated zone of active growth. In practical terms, this means that most of the strong new growth of a pergola-grown plant will be emerging from a very high level.

Those who prune *any* rose plant *must* be aware of the location of the zone of active growth on a given cane. Experienced pruners can apply that knowledge to a given pruning task.

Try to keep the zone of active growth as low as possible. Try to prune back to the strongest, newest growth that reaches all the way to the center of the structure.

BEWARE OF EXHAUSTED-NODE SYNDROME!

There is a chapter in this book that is entitled "Exhausted-Node Syndrome." I recommend that you read that chapter before you proceed with this section. Many arches and most pergolas have elevated zones of active growth. Exhausted-node syndrome occurs in most roses that have elevated zones of active growth. Folks who prune arches and pergolas should expect to find exhausted nodes.

Exhausted nodes should be removed, *if* strong, new growth is emerging from a lower point. This will reinvigorate both the cane and the plant.

LEAVE LONG STUBS

There is a chapter in this book that is entitled "Long Stubs Are Ugly but Beneficial." I recommend that you read that chapter before you proceed with this section.

Leave long stubs when you prune canes of any type, *especially* ones that are very thick.

A FEW WORDS ABOUT GROWING AND PRUNING ARCHES

Rose arches are joyous things. They embody many of the most endearing traits of their larger cousins (the pergolas) but on a smaller scale. That smaller part works for most of us; we are not getting any younger.

The criteria for selecting suitable varieties for growing on arches are a little more relaxed. Arches are generally much smaller structures than are pergolas. Smaller structures require smaller plants as covers. This means that varieties can be selected that will grow a single new cane that reaches from ground level to the middle of the arch. Canes do not have to build onto each other to reach the middle of the arch.

This is liberating for both the grower and the rose. Zones of active growth can be maintained at low levels. Plants can be pruned so that their canes are replaced every two or three years.

PRUNE DOWN

There are two main methods by which arches and pillars are pruned. The most common method is the most obvious: the pruner stands on a ladder or the pergola structure. Those methods are dangerous. Most arches and pergolas were designed to support plants not people. That leaves you and the ladders. Ladders will kill you, if they can.

I design my garden structures to be pruned. I leave large, open spaces on the plant-supporting surfaces. This allows me to prune the plants from the sides and from below. When it is used properly, this technique is much safer than working from the top of the plants.

DON'T ALLOW ROSE CANES TO BECOME SAW BLADES!

Rose canes are like saw blades. They have teeth scattered around their circumference. It is quite tempting to cut a cane at the bottom, and then pull it out of the plant. Don't do that! The prickles (thorns) of the canes will cut neighboring growth.

Cut canes into several, smaller pieces. You can then safely remove them without hurting the plant.

It is especially important that you use this cane-removal method when you prune a plant from below.

Garden Safety

• • •

Make yourself
A stronger thing,
Gird your body, true.
Make gloves,
And boots,
And eye-save glasses
Companions when you hew.

Hard work

Gardening is a form of a manual labor. It is accomplished with muscle and sinew, not gasoline and electricity. The human body is more difficult to repair than a power tool. The human body also lacks the endurance of power tools. We must protect our bodies. This will minimize the damage that is done to them when we work in the garden.

Personal safety equipment

I wear a uniform when I work in the garden: long denim pants, long-sleeved shirt, stout boots, a hat with side shields, and gloves. Winter, summer—everyday, I wear those clothes.

Accessories come and go from my gardening wardrobe ensemble. For example, I wear an unlined, long-sleeve denim jacket when I prune roses and fruit trees. I call it my flak jacket. Denim jackets will deter many prickles—if you are careful.

When I climb ladders, I wear work boots that are equipped with a strong, internal shank. This lessens the possibility that I will strain the arches of my feet.

I wear nitrile gloves for normal work that does not involve roses. When I work with roses, I wear leather gloves. Make sure to buy gloves that *entirely* cover the fingers with leather.

Caution! Do not use canvas-backed gloves to work on roses! Such gloves offer minimal protection against rose prickles!

Caution! Do not use the gloves that you use on roses for general labor! The gloves can be thinned by general tasks that do not involve roses. This can lead to dangerous punctures on the hands!

Caution! Do not use leather gloves that have become wet! Wet leather gloves can be easily penetrated by rose prickles!

Wear safety goggles when you work in the garden. I know that this sounds vaguely overprotective, but it's not. Eye injuries are no fun.

Wear hearing protection, when you work with noisy equipment.

Wear a good-quality respirator when you work in dusty conditions.

Ladders are dangerous!

Working on ladders is always a dangerous activity. Using ladders out in the garden or on other uneven surfaces is off the scale, in terms of danger. No rose plant, no garden is worth being killed or injured for the sake of maintenance.

If you must grow taller plants, use an appropriate type of ladder.

If you must use a ladder, be safe.

Caution! Don't use general-purpose ladders outdoors! Use ladders that are engineered and certified for agricultural use.

Work strong; work safe

There is an old saying that goes like this: "There is always something to do on a farm." Never were truer words spoken. Farm and garden work never ends.

Garden work is cyclical. It changes with the seasons. That provides variety for your mind and body. But changing work means changing muscles. You need to acclimate your body to the changing nature of your gardening jobs.

I only prune two or three hours per day at the beginning of the season. My muscles and tendons aren't in pruning shape, early on.

I'm usually in great pruning shape in late December. That's when I begin to schedule my off-site pruning jobs. When I'm in shape, I can justify a day spent pruning someone else's garden. I know that I won't tire out by lunch.

CALL IT A DAY, BEFORE YOU BECOME TOO TIRED

Race horses love to run. Gardeners love to work in the garden. Sometimes horses and people don't know when to quit. That's when they get hurt.

Clean up and go inside, before you become too tired. This will help to prevent mistakes you will regret for a very long time.

A Nearly Lost Form of Tree Rose

● ● ●

Go softly now,
The creeping dusk
Falling on a gift.
Once sorely given
(Aptly received!)
None care to pass it on…
Cascade Roses.

EVERY STORY HAS A BEGINNING; EVERY GOOD THING MEETS ITS END

I AM THE FINAL LINK in a chain that stretches across two continents and several hundred years. How did that sad eventuality come to pass? Ah, but that part makes for an interesting tale.

Like so many things in our modern world, it began with a telephone conversation. The caller was a ninety-two-year-old woman named Ramona Stocking. Ramona told me she needed someone to prune her roses.

Ramona was an interesting person. Her grandfathers were among the first Anglo settlers in the Santa Clara Valley. Ramona's grandfathers acquired huge tracts of land. They became quite wealthy. Two major streets in San Jose are named after Ramona's grandfathers (McKee Road and Lundy Avenue).

Ramona was the product of a rigid Victorian upbringing. A popular rubric of the time indicated "idle hands are the devil's workshop."

Ramona's parents used that maxim as a goad to ensure that their children were *anything* but idle. Ramona and her siblings studied, prayed, and worked (and worked, worked, *worked*).

Ramona took her parents' work-oriented outlook to heart. Most women of the day became housewives. In 1929, Ramona founded a rose nursery with her husband, Clyde Stocking.

The nursery prospered. That was no small feat. The Great Depression of the 1920s and '30s was in full swing. Ramona said, "If someone only had ten cents in their pocket, they would buy a rose plant, instead of a loaf of bread. They knew that the bread would be gone tomorrow. The plant would give them joy for years to come."

Ramona had an eye for roses. Clyde was an innovative businessman and industry leader. They were a formidable team. Clyde and Ramona Stocking were pillars of the American rose business.

Ramona was no stranger to me. I had been a customer of the Stocking Rose nursery for several years. Our past meetings had been stiff, formal things. That's the way it usually goes, when rose legends meet young aspirants to the cause.

But our first meeting in the world of rose labor was a far different thing; it took Ramona and me about ten minutes to fall in love with each other. Ramona said, "You prune roses just like my deceased husband, Clyde. He was the best. I never met another person who pruned roses *his* way."

Ramona's compliments were appreciated. Most people complain about the way I prune roses. Some think I prune the plants too harshly. The majority believe I don't prune the plants low enough. Then and now, I prune roses in a manner that I believe is best for the individual plants (and the safety of the garden).

At noon, Ramona announced that she was going inside to eat lunch. I said that I would eat my sandwich out in the garden. Ramona said, "Oh, my! That will *never* do. You must come inside and have lunch with *us*."

I soon found out who Ramona meant by "us." First was George Haight. George ran the rose nursery for Ramona. He had worked in the Stocking Rose Nursery since about 1945. He was Clyde Stocking's right-hand man for fifteen years. HeGeorge the nursery for 30 years after Clyde's death. George Haight knew *everything* about selling and growing roses.

Shirley Cohn and Roselle Goldman rounded out that inaugural lunch. Shirley ran the office in a capable way. Roselle was a single mother who helped in the nursery, when she could. Roselle was a great friend.

Ramona led the group into her house. She directed me toward the large breakfast nook that was located on one side of the kitchen. The nook jutted out into Ramona's garden. The windows overlooked the display yard of the rose nursery. A large bed of tree peonies was growing just outside of the windows. Ramona explained that her grandmother had brought the plants across the continent in a covered wagon.

I realized that the view from that window hadn't changed since about 1930. I knew enough about history to realize that the view from that window would not have been out of place *in* 1830!

Ramona learned her manners in the nineteenth century. She knew how to steer a conversation. Ramona was curious why I knew so much about plants at such a young age. (I was thirty-one.)

I explained that I was raised around orchards and fields. I had an innate, natural genius for fruit trees. When I was three years old, I could identify every type of stone fruit tree—even when they were dormant.

I told Ramona that my innate horticultural talent was tempered with hard work. She was surprised when I told her that I began working in other people's gardens when I was just eleven. I needed the money to buy food—and toys.

Ramona perked up, and then got a little sad, when I told her those things. She said, "Ah, but there's another way that you are like Clyde Stocking. He was forced to work when he was quite young." She was still pining for her lost husband, twenty years after his death.

After lunch, Ramona told me that George was recovering from cardiac surgery. She asked me if I would assist George Haight in the rose nursery. He needed the help of an experienced rosarian.

It took me about two seconds to say yes. I didn't even ask about the salary. I wanted to work on that nineteenth-century relic farm. I wanted to learn from Ramona and George. I also wanted to learn how to become a nurseryman. The Stocking Rose Nursery was the right place to learn that trade.

The nursery grounds covered thirteen acres. The rear portion of the property was planted with rows of rose plants. The main compound was a maze of ramshackle sheds, old trucks, antique tractors, farm equipment, and dirt roads.

A hundred-foot-long pile of redwood stakes stood off to one side of the tractor shed. Ramona explained that they were leftovers from the days when the Stockings produced thousands of tree roses. Some of the stakes were almost hundred years old. They were cut from two-thousand-year-old coast redwood trees. I wish that I had those stakes, today. I would find something to do with them.

Containerized plant-growing grounds were dotted around the nursery. Rose plants of every description were growing in various states of sad decrepitude. George knew everything about rose growing—but he was a careless nurseryman.

Giants stood in the middle of George's sad little roses. He grew tree roses that stood over ten feet tall. They had thick, gnarled, eight-foot tall trunks. Their canopies were six-feet wide and tall. They were the size of small fruit trees.

I was amazed. I had never seen such a thing. I immediately sought out George and asked him about the gigantic tree roses I saw out in the growing yard. He said, "Oh, Tom. Those are called 'cascades.' They used to be much more common than they are, now." George went on and said, "I lose money on those silly things. I only grow them because I *have* to."

I asked George what he meant, when he said, "I *have* to."

He said, "Clyde Stocking taught me how to grow cascades. He was taught to grow them by Father George Schoener. He was taught by somebody in Europe. So, you see, Tom, it goes back hundreds of years." George hit me with the *real* punch line. He said, "I'm the only person in North America who is still growing eight-foot cascades. I don't want to see them die out."

I stood there, gaping. I was stunned by the beauty and history of George's cascades. I was *very* stunned that George was willing to teach me how to grow them.

George Haight worked me like a rented mule for almost three years. He taught me the fundamentals of the rose business. I also learned how to be a first-class rose farmer. Best of all, I got to improve my pruning skills. I added the nursery's huge rose garden to the long list of places I pruned. I loved working with Ramona's ancient plants.

In my off-duty hours, I grew roses in my own nursery. That school of hard knocks provided me with a series of rigid, unforgiving lessons. It was hard, rough work. But I was playing with plants. That's all that mattered.

My adventures away from the Stocking nursery brought me into contact with many old-line professional rose and fruit-tree growers. There were a lot of old people who were willing to teach a young man how to grow roses, back then. It was an exclusive little club. I seemed to be the only one who was interested to hear what most of them had to say.

Ralph Moore was *the* exception to the general loneliness I found among older rose growers. People of all ages sought Ralph out for his knowledge. Everyone else was forgotten, except by their families.

Much of what George Haight taught me about rose growing was *wrong*. He was a horrible nurseryman. George was sick of roses. George was sick of rose fanatics. He was *very* sick of working sixty-hour weeks.

I know there was an emotional side to George's malaise. George Haight was no Clyde Stocking. That was a widely known fact. I believe he was tired of living in the great man's shadow.

George Haight taught me how to grow roses the *wrong* way. Dr. Leonard Covell, Gene Dana, Frank De Fiore, Charles "Chuck" Elliott Jr., Dennison "Denny" Morey, Ralph Moore, Miriam Wilkins, and Ramona Stocking taught me how to grow roses the *right* way.

This is the process by which I became the last classically trained, full-spectrum rosarian who will ever be produced in America. I know that this is true. The mechanism to create more like me has been dismantled. The great rose nurseries have vanished. Most of the cut-flower greenhouses are gone. The great rosarians are dead. The rose-growing hobby is dead.

So, it is that I became the last of an ancient kind. My exile is made poignant by *this* statistic; there used to be ten of me in every generation. I count myself as being fortunate to have known several of that last great crop of American rosarians. I am sad that I am their only successor.

Some might argue that the rose greats of today are the living equivalents of the people I met from the 1950s through the 1980s. That is pure hogwash. The rose growers of today offer pale imitations of the greatness that once existed in the various branches of the American rose industry.

In my opinion, Stephen Scanniello is the only exception to the lack of greatness that exists among current American rosarians. Stephen is a fantastic gardener.

The men and women who taught me knew *everything* about their craft. They possessed knowledge that had been passed down to them by the pioneers of the nursery business. They collaborated with the greatest rose hybridizers of all time.

My mentors had the experience of centuries under their belts. They earned their keep by growing and selling roses in ways that are now gone. Most of those rose-growing ways don't make economic sense in today's globalized world. But the horticultural excellence of their methods was second to none. Plants will be plants, folks. They will always require the same things.

In their off-hours, my teachers went home to work in their own gardens. They lived the rose.

Some of my teachers weren't publicly acknowledged as being rose greats. They were laborers. My second rose budder (a person who grafts roses) was named Paul Begonia. Paul was close to eighty years old when he began to work for me. By that time, he had been working with roses for better than sixty years. Paul worked with most of the American great rosarians of the early twentieth century. He was a wonderful teacher of rose knowledge and history.

A NEARLY LOST FORM OF TREE ROSE

People ask me why I still grow giant tree roses. Yes, I know. They are difficult to propagate. Yes, I know, they are hellishly complicated to train and prune. What am I saying? Cascades are *dangerous* to prune.

I suppose I have become a little like George Haight. No, not the careless nurseryman part. I take my craft *quite* seriously. I am like George in the "I *have* to grow them" part.

Cascades possess a unique and incomparable form of garden beauty. Grand European ladies of olden times were aware of that quality. Old Lithographs depict garden courtyards that are sprinkled with tall, drooping cascade roses. The cascades make larger parasols above the ladies' smaller ones.

I have had a lot of fun growing cascades. I went far beyond the techniques and varietal repertoire of Clyde Stocking and George Haight. I have enjoyed fabulous successes and inglorious failures in my quest to improve cascades.

At one time, I propagated and sold more than three hundred eight-foot cascades, each year. I even put them into twelve-foot-long boxes and shipped them across the continent. Yes, in 1996, lots of people were willing to a thousand dollars to get one of my rose plants shipped to their gardens!

WHAT NEXT?

There was a time wherein I lived a fantasy; I hoped aspirants for my knowledge would eventually appear. Then I remembered the lonely old men and women with whom I spent countless hours. They were great people, yet they received few visitors. Fewer still came to learn from their unique experiences.

I am not going to write about the mechanics of growing cascades. Why? Few American gardeners will grow the things. The human demographic for developing enthusiasm for cascades is not good. The percentage of people who possess garden knowledge is declining. Young people today are watchers, not doers. They are voyeurs of the truest kind.

Cascades are hellishly difficult to propagate, grow, train and maintain. You need to be a master rosarian to propagate and maintain cascades. I have met few of those, as of late (aside from you, dear Stephen Scanniello). I don't expect aging rosarians to climb ladders so that they can propagate, grow, and maintain cascades.

My advice to people who want to see cascade roses is simple; go to Europe. I'm told that they have people there who still cherish their gardening traditions. In any case, cascades are more common in Europe than they are in America.

No, I'm not going to write about cascades. At best, my words might provide an interesting day's reading. They would be forgotten just as quickly.

But there are worse things than being forgotten. Many folks have asked me questions. Some have publicly repeated my answers as if they were their own. Others have taken credit for what I have done. I don't care to have a repeat of that dynamic with my rarest bit of knowledge: cascade roses. They belong to me.

On the other hand, I don't care to break a chain of continuity that stretches back hundreds of years. Yes, I know; when I die, that chain will probably be severed. But I won't be around to realize the fact. Until then, I will enjoy my own cascades. Their kind is no less lovely to my eyes now, than they were thirty-six years ago.

So, it is that crafts are lost. So, it is that traditions are lost. So, it is that cultures are lost.

Tom Liggett. The one and *only* founder of the San Jose Heritage Rose Garden.

June 21, 2017.

GLOSSARY

The following terms are ones that I have heard, learned, invented, or adapted for my own use. Some of these terms are archaic. Many are "old friends," which feel correct in how they describe a given thing or activity.

Apical dominance. The process by which a plant's central stem becomes more dominant than its side stems.

Aseptic technique. 1. Methods for maintaining sterile conditions. 2. Techniques that avoid the spread of infectious organisms between living things.

Auxins. Naturally occurring chemicals that coordinate the growth and behavior of plants.

Basal break. A strong new cane that originates from the very bottom of a grafted or own-root rose. In the case of a grafted plant, this term applies only to a cane of the grafted or named variety, *not* to any suckers, which originate from the rootstock. See "sucker" elsewhere in this glossary.

Break. 1. A new rose shoot. 2. To grow.

Broken. A growth bud that is no longer dormant but has started growing. See "dormant eye" elsewhere in this glossary.

Bud. 1. Buds are the portion of a rose plant that breaks (sprouts) and grows to make a new stem or cane (also called an "eye"). 2. The part of a rose that is used to bud another plant to asexually propagate it. 3. The act of budding a plant (to bud it). 4. A new or young bloom.

Bud union. 1. The point where the eye was budded onto the shank of the rootstock. 2. The point from which all new basal breaks will initially originate.

Cane (rose). The basal break or principal stem of a rose. See "basal break" elsewhere in this glossary.

Canes of the year. 1. An archaic term. 2. A stem, cane, or basal break that was produced during the current growing season. 3. A stem, cane, or basal break that is less than a year old.

Canestock. 1. A single very long cane that has been grown to produce a tree rose. 2. The trunk of a tree rose. 3. A canestock is a type of interstock.

Cascade. Tree roses that have a canestock (trunk) that is at least four feet tall. See "canestock" elsewhere in this glossary.

China (*Rosa chinensis*, China rose). 1. A specific type of rose that originated in China. Chinas were pivotal in the development of repeat-blooming modern cultivars. 2. A variety that is widely accepted as possessing sufficient *R. chinensis* traits to be included in the China class of roses.

Climber, climbers. 1. A class of roses that produces very long canes. 2. There are two main types of climbers: pillar-type and traditional climbers. 3. Traditional climbers produce floricanes. They not bloom on the new canes of the year. Traditional climbers produce blooms on their canes during the second and subsequent years. 4. Pillar-type climbers produce primocanes. They bloom on the new canes of the year. See "pillar-type climbers" elsewhere in this glossary. See "canes of the year" elsewhere in this glossary. See "floricane" and "primocane" elsewhere in this glossary.

Dead zone (nutrient dead zone). The blank portion of a rose stem that lies directly behind a growth bud.

De-facto hybrid teas. Floribundas and grandifloras are being bred to produce hybrid tea-type blooms. That look is required to win prizes in formal competitions. Most of the differences that once existed between the hybrid teas, floribundas, and grandifloras have gradually disappeared. Floribundas and grandifloras have become de-facto hybrid teas.

Disinfecting/disinfection process. 1. The act of disinfecting or cleansing a cutting tool to reduce the possibility that diseases will be spread. 2. Disinfect cutting tools when you have finished work with a given variety. 3. Dip cutting tools in 70 percent or 90 percent isopropyl (rubbing) alcohol. Operate shears a few times. Wipe off excess alcohol with a clean paper towel. 4. Soak used reciprocating-saw blades in 70 percent or 90 percent isopropyl (rubbing) alcohol, and clean with a wire brush.

Doc Farwell's. A line of products used in grafting plants. Also, used to repair damaged plants. This is the *only* product that is recommended by the author in this book. I do not normally do testimonials. I have never received benefit for providing a testimonial.

Dogleg. The portion of a rose cane that arcs away from the main stem.

Dormant (dormancy). A period when a bud or plant is not growing but is still viable. In roses the normal period of dormancy (or semi dormancy) occurs when the days are short.

Dormant eyes. Growth buds that have not broken (sprouted).

Enzymes. Naturally occurring chemicals that accelerate or catalyze chemical reactions in living organisms.

Exhausted-node syndrome. 1. A term that was coined by Tom Liggett. 2. Exhausted-node syndrome refers to a condition wherein nodes cease to produce high-quality breaks.

Exhibiting, exhibition (rose). 1. The process of entering roses in formal, organized amateur rose shows to win prizes. 2. Exhibiting roses for prizes began in England in the 1860s.

Exhibition standard (rose). 1. A generally arbitrary set of criteria that a bloom must have to win prizes in formal, organized rose shows. 2. The exhibition standard has sometimes driven how roses look and what varieties were introduced.

Eye (eyes). A synonymous term for bud. See "bud" elsewhere in this glossary.

Floricane. A type of cane that does not generally produce flowers during its first year of growth. See "primocane" elsewhere in this glossary.

Growth eye. See "bud" elsewhere in this glossary.

Growth hormones. See "auxins" elsewhere in this glossary.

Heading back. The act of cutting a new break so that it will produce side shoots instead of a single cane.

Hippocratic oath. 1. An ancient Greek code oath that pertains to medical ethics. 2. A general concept that dictates that caregivers should not harm their charges through neglect or overtreatment. 3. It is the author's opinion that the Hippocratic oath can also be applied to the care of living plants.

Inflorescence. A set of blooms that are borne on a single stem or cane.

Interstock. See "canestock" elsewhere in this glossary.

Log stage; log stage of rose-plant growth. 1. Newly propagated rose plants have three stages of growth: lag, log lag. 2. The first lag stage is characterized by slow plant growth. 3. When plants are in their log stage, they are growing at a semi logarithmic pace. In common terms, this means the plants grow explosively. Plants that are in a log stage are growing at a semi logarithmic pace. It is easier to say that plants that are growing at a semi logarithmic pace are in a log stage. 3. Somewhere around the third to fifth year, after they were rooted or budded, most roses stop growing in a semi logarithmic fashion. This is the beginning of the second lag stage of growth.

Lopping shears (also called "loppers"). 1. A pair of pruning shears that is designed to be used with two hands. 2. Handle lengths generally vary from twelve to thirty-six inches in length. 3. Lopping shears can cut much larger wood than hand shears. 4. Lopping shears generally make a cleaner, safer cut that is better for the plant that is being pruned. 5. Lopping shears reduce human muscle strains and repetitive-use injuries when they are used to make cuts that are greater than a half inch in diameter.

Node. 1. In roses, the place where a leaf grows during the first year that a new stem was produced is called a "node." Nodes contain undifferentiated growth cells. "Undifferentiated" means that the cells have not yet "decided" whether they will grow downward and become roots or upward and become leaves, stems, and flowers. 2. All new growth in rose plants originates from a node of one form or another. See "exhausted-node syndrome" elsewhere in the glossary of terms.

Organic. A material that occurs naturally.

Overgrown plant. A rose plant that has elevated its zone of active growth six inches or more above the original level. See "zone of active growth" elsewhere in this glossary.

Own root (own-rooted, own-root plants). Plants that are propagated from cuttings, not by grafting.

Pillar. A rose plant that is grown as a tall, narrow column. Pillars are generally tied to stakes or other vertical support mechanisms.

Pillar-type climber. 1. Pillar-type climbers produce primocanes. They bloom on the new canes of the year.2. A very tall bush that is classed as a climber. See "canes of the year" elsewhere in this glossary. See "climber" elsewhere in this glossary. See "floricane" and "primocane" elsewhere in this glossary.

Plant politicians. 1. People who go to lots of meetings and feel the need to hold office in plant societies. 2. Many plant politicians don't work in the garden very much. 3. Many plant politicians like to tell *real* gardeners how to grow plants.

Prickles. Rose thorns.

Primocane. A cane that produces flowers during its first year of growth. See "floricane" elsewhere in this glossary.

Pruning for plant replacement. A pruning technique that encourages rose plants to replace their old canes with new ones.

Religion (rose). 1. The act of suspending science and logic in favor of emotional or popular beliefs. 2. Blindly accepting what everybody knows over scientific inquiry and fact. See "plant politicians" elsewhere in this glossary.

Rootstock. 1. A plant that is grown for use in grafting. 2. The roots of a grafted plant. Note on definition number two: the scion portion of a grafted plant sometimes produces roots. When this happens, the roots of the former rootstock will sometimes become subsumed (overwhelmed).

Rose grower's disease. See "Sporotrichosis" elsewhere in this glossary.

Rose politics. 1. Being involved with roses for any reason other than the love of the plant. 2. The act of placing more importance on winning prizes, holding office, gaining control of gardens or gardening organizations than securing the welfare of rose plants. 3. Promoting one type of rose or flower type to the exclusion of others. See "plant politicians" elsewhere in this glossary.

Rose politicians. People who engage in rose politics.

Semi logarithmic stage of growth. See "log stage of growth" elsewhere in this glossary.

Sporotrichosis (rose grower's disease). 1. *Sphagnum* moss contains the spores of *Sporotrichosis schenckii*. This organism generally affects the skin, but can also infect the lungs, bones, joints, or brain. The name of the disease it causes is Sporotrichosis or rose grower's disease. 2. Anyone who works with *Sphagnum* (peat) moss should do so in an informed and safe manner.

Sport. A plant mutation. 1. Growth sports produce plants which are larger or smaller than the original variety. 2. Color sports produce blooms that vary in color from the original variety. 3. Some sports are unstable. They sport to new variations or revert to the original variety.

Spurs. A type of side shoot that produces flowers.

Stake. A long piece of metal, plastic or wood that is used to support plants.

Staking. A process by which plants are supported with stakes.

Standard (tree rose). A rose plant that is grafted at the very top of a long, single canestock (trunk) to create a lollypop or fountain effect. Frequently budded at about twenty-four inches (mini tree) or thirty-six inches (standard tree rose). Rarely budded by enthusiasts at six or eight feet to produce a cascade or weeping tree rose. See "tree rose" elsewhere in this glossary. See "cascade" elsewhere in this glossary.

Stove wood canes. Rose canes that have become very old.

Stub. The portion of a stem that remains above a bud after pruning.

Sucker, suckers. Undesirable growth that originates from the rootstock of a grafted plant. See "rootstock" elsewhere in this glossary.

Suckering. 1. A grafted plant that is producing suckers from the root-stock. 2. The process by which suckers are removed from a plant. See "sucker" elsewhere in this glossary.

Sulk, sulking. Rose plants that are pruned improperly sometimes lose vigor.

Synthetic. A material that is man-made.

Tea (tea rose). 1. *Rosa odorata*, one of the ancestral types of roses that were brought to Europe in the late eighteenth century. 2. Later hybrids of *Rosa odorata*. See *Rosa odorata* elsewhere in this glossary.

Tender. 1. When a rose is killed or damaged by temperatures at or slightly below freezing, then it is said to be tender. 2. A variety is said to be tender when it will not withstand freezing weather.

Thorns. See "prickles" elsewhere in this glossary.

Tying material. Any fibrous material that is used to tie rose plants.

Tying. 1. Using fibrous materials to tie rose plants. 2. Using budding strips to secure grafts.

Tree rose. (standard). A rose plant that is grafted at the very top of a long, single canestock (trunk) to create a lollypop or fountain effect. Frequently budded at about twenty-four inches (mini tree) or thirty-six inches (standard tree rose). Extremely rarely budded by enthusiasts at six or eight feet to produce a cascade or weeping tree rose. See "standard tree rose" elsewhere in this glossary. See "cascade" elsewhere in this glossary.

Vigor (rose). The amount of enthusiasm with which a rose grows is a measure of its vigor. Two three-foot plants of the same variety might not grow and bloom as well as the other. The one that does is said to be more vigorous.

Virus (rose). A microscopic organism that consists of DNA with a protein coat. Many viruses are highly contagious and are harmful to roses.

Virused (rose). Plants that are infected with one or more viruses.

Winter protection. Any activity that is used as protection against freezing or variable winter weather.

Zone of active growth. 1. The area of a plant from which the greater part of any strong, new growth originates. 2. With newly rooted rose plants, the zone of active growth will be at or just below the surface of the soil. 3. With newly budded rose plants, the zone of active growth will be at the bud union.

41414983R00083

Made in the USA
Middletown, DE
07 April 2019